Ancient Texts and the Bible
Book 7 - Easy Reader Edition

Israel...
From Sinai to the Tabernacle

Minister 2 Others

Ancient Texts and the Bible
Book 7

Israel...
From Sinai to the Tabernacle

Easy Reader Edition

Israel... From Sinai to the Tabernacle
ISBN 978-1-947751-25-5

Minister2others.com

Ancient texts compiled for this series:

The Bible
King James Version 1769

The Book of Enoch
An English translation by Dr. Laurence,
Archbishop of Cashel,
Formerly Professor of Hebrew at Oxford, 1833

The Book of Jasher
Faithfully translated 1840
from the original Hebrew into English
Published by J.H. Parry & Company 1887

The Book of Jubilees
by R.H. Charles, Oxford: Clarendon Press, 1913

Ancient Texts and the Bible

series include:

Book 1: In The Beginning... From Adam to Noah

Book 2: In The Beginning... From Noah to Abraham

Book 3: In The Beginning... From Abraham to Israel

Book 4: In The Beginning... From Israel to Egypt

Book 5: In The Beginning... From Egypt to Goshen

Book 6: Israel... From Goshen to Sinai

Book 7: Israel... From Sinai to the Tabernacle

Book 8: Israel... Through the Book of Leviticus

Book 9: Israel... Through the Book of Numbers

Book 10: Israel... Through the Book of Joshua

Table of Contents:

Forward

The **Ancient Texts and the Bible** series synchronizes the manuscripts of Enoch, Jasher, and Jubilees into the Bible, making one complete storyline. The books are interwoven using the Torah as the backbone, and the extra-biblical texts as the fleshing out of that backbone.

The seventh book in this series contains Exodus chapters 21-40, the book of Jasher parts of chapters 82, and the book of Jubilees chapter 1.

Though the language in the writings have been updated, replacing words like "*thou*" and "*thine*" with words like "*you*" and "*your*", the integrity of the verses remain.

The "*Easy Reader*" edition is for those who just want to read the storyline and enjoy the journey. The stop signs and complex formatting have been removed so one may merely focus upon the story being told.

The *Expanded Edition* of **Ancient Texts and the Bible** was created for the more studious reader. The various manuscripts have the following formatting applied to them in this edition:

the Bible - Regular

THE BOOK OF ENOCH - ALL CAPITALS

the Book of Jasher - Italics

<u>the Book of Jubilees - Underlined</u>

Where one of the extra-biblical texts reiterates the Bible, the phrase is then put in a **bold font**. Where two manuscripts overlap each other exclusive of the Bible, then both fonts are used. For instance, where Jasher and Jubilees intercept, the text is then formatted as *Italics and Underlined.*

The stop sign is another element to the *Expanded Edition* that is not seen in the *Easy Reader*. This image points to contradictions in the content. Printed versions also contain page numbers within the stop sign revealing the page where contradictory information is located, and vice versa. This information was not feasible to place in the e-book versions since the page numbers vary depending on the font size the reader chooses. Following, is an example from each edition:

Easy Reader Edition:

(Exodus 24:16) (Jasher 82:8...) (...Jubilees 1:2, 3...)
And the glory of the LORD abode upon mount Sinai, and the cloud covered it six days: and the seventh day he called to Moses out of the midst of the cloud.

Expanded Edition:

(Exodus 24:16) (Jasher 82:8...) (...Jubilees 1:2, 3...)
And the glory of the LORD abode upon mount Sinai, and the cloud covered it six days: and the seventh day he called to Moses out of the midst of the cloud.

Whichever you choose, may you ***Enjoy the Journey***!

Exodus: Chapter Twenty-One

(Exodus 21:1)
Now these are the judgments which you shall set before them.

(Exodus 21:2)
If you buy an Hebrew servant, six years he shall serve: and in the seventh he shall go out free for nothing.

(Exodus 21:3)
If he came in by himself, he shall go out by himself: if he were married, then his wife shall go out with him.

(Exodus 21:4)
If his master has given him a wife, and she have born him sons or daughters; the wife and her children shall be her master's, and he shall go out by himself.

(Exodus 21:5)
And if the servant shall plainly say, I love my master, my wife, and my children; I will not go out free:

(Exodus 21:6)
Then his master shall bring him to the judges; he shall also bring him to the door, or to the door post; and his master shall bore his ear through with an aul; and he shall serve him forever.

(Exodus 21:7)
And if a man sale his daughter to be a maidservant, she shall not go out as the menservants do.

(Exodus 21:8)

If she please not her master, who has betrothed her to himself, then shall he let her be redeemed: to sell her to a strange nation he shall have no power, seeing he has dealt deceitfully with her.

(Exodus 21:9)

And if he has betrothed her to his son, he shall deal with her after the manner of daughters.

(Exodus 21:10)

If he takes him another wife; her food, her raiment, and her duty of marriage, shall he not diminish.

(Exodus 21:11)

And if he does not these three to her, then shall she go out free without money.

(Exodus 21:12)

He that smites a man, so that he dies, shall be surely put to death.

(Exodus 21:13)

And if a man lies not in wait, but God deliver him into his hand; then I will appoint you a place whither he shall flee.

(Exodus 21:14)

But if a man come presumptuously upon his neighbor, to slay him with guile; you shall take him from mine altar, that he may die.

(Exodus 21:15)

And he that smites his father, or his mother, shall be surely put to death.

(Exodus 21:16)

And he that steals a man, and sales him, or if he be found in his hand, he shall surely be put to death.

(Exodus 21:17)

And he that curses his father, or his mother, shall surely be put to death.

(Exodus 21:18)

And if men strive together, and one smite another with a stone, or with his fist, and he dies not, but keeps his bed:

(Exodus 21:19)

If he rises again, and walk abroad upon his staff, then shall he that smote him be quit: only he shall pay for the loss of his time, and shall cause him to be thoroughly healed.

(Exodus 21:20)

And if a man smites his servant, or his maid, with a rod, and he die under his hand; he shall be surely punished.

(Exodus 21:21)

Notwithstanding, if he continues a day or two, he shall not be punished: for he is his money.

(Exodus 21:22)

If men strive, and hurt a woman with child, so that her fruit depart from her, and yet no mischief follow: he shall be surely punished, according as the woman's husband will lay upon him; and he shall pay as the judges determine.

(Exodus 21:23)

And if any mischief follows, then you shall give life for life,

(Exodus 21:24)

Eye for eye, tooth for tooth, hand for hand, foot for foot,

(Exodus 21:25)

Burning for burning, wound for wound, stripe for stripe.

(Exodus 21:26)

And if a man smites the eye of his servant, or the eye of his maid, that it perish; he shall let him go free for his eye's sake.

(Exodus 21:27)

And if he smites out his manservant's tooth, or his maidservant's tooth; he shall let him go free for his tooth's sake.

(Exodus 21:28)

If an ox gores a man or a woman, that they die: then the ox shall be surely stoned, and his flesh shall not be eaten; but the owner of the ox shall be quit.

(Exodus 21:29)

But if the ox were wont to push with his horn in time past, and it has been testified to his owner, and he has not kept him in, but that he has killed a man or a woman; the ox shall be stoned, and his owner also shall be put to death.

(Exodus 21:30)

If there be laid on him a sum of money, then he shall give for the ransom of his life whatsoever is laid upon him.

(Exodus 21:31)

Whether he have gored a son, or have gored a daughter, according to this judgment shall it be done to him.

(Exodus 21:32)

If the ox shall push a manservant or a maidservant; he shall give to their master thirty shekels of silver, and the ox shall be stoned.

(Exodus 21:33)

And if a man shall open a pit, or if a man shall dig a pit, and not cover it, and an ox or an donkey fall therein;

(Exodus 21:34)

The owner of the pit shall make it good, and give money to the owner of them; and the dead beast shall be his.

(Exodus 21:35)

And if one man's ox hurt another's, that he dies; then they shall sell the live ox, and divide the money of it; and the dead ox also they shall divide.

(Exodus 21:36)

Or if it be known that the ox has used to push in time past, and his owner has not kept him in; he shall surely pay ox for ox; and the dead shall be his own.

Exodus: Chapter Twenty-Two

(Exodus 22:1)

If a man shall steal an ox, or a sheep, and kill it, or sell it; he shall restore five oxen for an ox, and four sheep for a sheep.

(Exodus 22:2)

If a thief be found breaking up, and be smitten that he dies, there shall no blood be shed for him.

(Exodus 22:3)

If the sun be risen upon him, there shall be blood shed for him; for he should make full restitution; if he has nothing, then he shall be sold for his theft.

(Exodus 22:4)

If the theft be certainly found in his hand alive, whether it be ox, or donkey, or sheep; he shall restore double.

(Exodus 22:5)

If a man shall cause a field or vineyard to be eaten, and shall put in his beast, and shall feed in another man's field; of the best of his own field, and of the best of his own vineyard, shall he make restitution.

(Exodus 22:6)

If fire break out, and catch in thorns, so that the stacks of corn, or the standing corn, or the field, be consumed therewith; he that kindled the fire shall surely make restitution.

(Exodus 22:7)

If a man shall deliver to his neighbor money or stuff to keep, and it be stolen out of the man's house; if the thief be found, let him pay double.

(Exodus 22:8)

If the thief be not found, then the master of the house shall be brought to the judges, to see whether he have put his hand to his neighbor's goods.

(Exodus 22:9)

For all manner of trespass, whether it be for ox, for donkey, for sheep, for raiment, or for any manner of lost thing, which another challenges to be his, the cause of both parties shall come before the judges; and whom the judges shall condemn, he shall pay double to his neighbor.

(Exodus 22:10)

If a man delivers to his neighbor an donkey, or an ox, or a sheep, or any beast, to keep; and it die, or be hurt, or driven away, no man seeing it:

(Exodus 22:11)

Then shall an oath of the LORD be between them both, that he has not put his hand to his neighbor's goods; and the owner of it shall accept thereof, and he shall not make it good.

(Exodus 22:12)

And if it be stolen from him, he shall make restitution to the owner thereof.

(Exodus 22:13)

If it be torn in pieces, then let him bring it for witness, and he shall not make good that which was torn.

(Exodus 22:14)

And if a man borrows ought of his neighbor, and it be hurt, or die, the owner thereof being not with it, he shall surely make it good.

(Exodus 22:15)

But if the owner thereof be with it, he shall not make it good: if it be a hired thing, it came for his hire.

(Exodus 22:16)

And if a man entices a maid that is not betrothed, and lie with her, he shall surely endow her to be his wife.

(Exodus 22:17)

If her father utterly refuses to give her to him, he shall pay money according to the dowry of virgins.

(Exodus 22:18)

You shall not suffer a witch to live.

(Exodus 22:19)

Whosoever lies with a beast shall surely be put to death.

(Exodus 22:20)

He that sacrifices to any god, save to the LORD only, he shall be utterly destroyed.

(Exodus 22:21)

You shall neither vex a stranger, nor oppress him: for you were strangers in the land of Egypt.

(Exodus 22:22)

You shall not afflict any widow, or fatherless child.

(Exodus 22:23)

If you afflict them in any wise, and they cry at all to me, I will surely hear their cry;

(Exodus 22:24)

And my wrath shall wax hot, and I will kill you with the sword; and your wives shall be widows, and your children fatherless.

(Exodus 22:25)

If you lend money to any of my people that is poor by you, you shall not be to him as a usurer, neither shall you lay upon him usury.

(Exodus 22:26)

If you at all take your neighbor's raiment to pledge, you shall deliver it to him by that the sun goes down:

(Exodus 22:27)

For that is his covering only, it is his raiment for his skin: wherein shall he sleep? And it shall come to pass, when he cries to me, that I will hear; for I am gracious.

(Exodus 22:28)

You shall not revile the gods, nor curse the ruler of your people.

(Exodus 22:29)

You shall not delay to offer the first of your ripe fruits, and of your liquors: the firstborn of your sons shall you give to me.

(Exodus 22:30)

Likewise shall you do with your oxen, and with your sheep: seven days it shall be with his dam; on the eighth day you shall give it me.

(Exodus 22:31)

And you shall be holy men to me: neither shall you eat any flesh that is torn of beasts in the field; you shall cast it to the dogs.

Exodus: Chapter Twenty-Three

(Exodus 23:1)

You shall not raise a false report: put not your hand with the wicked to be an unrighteous witness.

(Exodus 23:2)

You shall not follow a multitude to do evil; neither shall you speak in a cause to decline after many to wrest judgment:

(Exodus 23:3)

Neither shall you countenance a poor man in his cause.

(Exodus 23:4)

If you meet your enemy's ox or his donkey going astray, you shall surely bring it back to him again.

(Exodus 23:5)

If you see the donkey of him that hates you lying under his burden, and would forbear to help him, you shall surely help with him.

(Exodus 23:6)

You shall not wrest the judgment of your poor in his cause.

(Exodus 23:7)

Keep you far from a false matter; and the innocent and righteous slay you not: for I will not justify the wicked.

(Exodus 23:8)

And you shall take no gift: for the gift blinds the wise, and perverts the words of the righteous.

(Exodus 23:9)

Also you shall not oppress a stranger: for you know the heart of a stranger, seeing you were strangers in the land of Egypt.

(Exodus 23:10)

And six years you shall sow your land, and shall gather in the fruits thereof:

(Exodus 23:11)

But the seventh year you shall let it rest and lie still; that the poor of your people may eat: and what they leave the beasts of the field shall eat. In like manner you shall deal with your vineyard, and with your olive yard.

(Exodus 23:12)

Six days you shall do your work, and on the seventh day you shall rest: that your ox and your donkey may rest, and the son of your handmaid, and the stranger, may be refreshed.

(Exodus 23:13)

And in all things that I have said to you be circumspect: and make no mention of the name of other gods, neither let it be heard out of your mouth.

(Exodus 23:14)

Three times you shall keep a feast to me in the year.

(Exodus 23:15)

You shall keep the feast of unleavened bread: (you shall eat unleavened bread seven days, as I commanded you, in the time appointed of the month Abib; for in it you came out from Egypt: and none shall appear before me empty:)

(Exodus 23:16)

And the feast of harvest, the firstfruits of your labors, which you have sown in the field: and the feast of ingathering, which is in the end of the year, when you have gathered in your labors out of the field.

(Exodus 23:17)

Three times in the year all your males shall appear before the Lord GOD.

(Exodus 23:18)

You shall not offer the blood of my sacrifice with leavened bread; neither shall the fat of my sacrifice remain until the morning.

(Exodus 23:19)

The first of the firstfruits of your land you shall bring into the house of the LORD your God. You shall not seethe a kid in his mother's milk.

(Exodus 23:20)

Behold, I send an Angel before you, to keep you in the way, and to bring you into the place which I have prepared.

(Exodus 23:21)

Beware of him, and obey his voice, provoke him not; for he will not pardon your transgressions: for my name is in him.

(Exodus 23:22)

But if you shall indeed obey his voice, and do all that I speak; then I will be an enemy to your enemies, and an adversary to your adversaries.

(Exodus 23:23)

For mine Angel shall go before you, and bring you in to the Amorites, and the Hittites, and the Perizzites, and the Canaanites, the Hivites, and the Jebusites: and I will cut them off.

(Exodus 23:24)

You shall not bow down to their gods, nor serve them, nor do after their works: but you shall utterly overthrow them, and quite break down their images.

(Exodus 23:25)

And you shall serve the LORD your God, and he shall bless your bread, and your water; and I will take sickness away from the midst of you.

(Exodus 23:26)

There shall nothing cast their young, nor be barren, in your land: the number of your days I will fulfill.

(Exodus 23:27)

I will send my fear before you, and will destroy all the people to whom you shall come, and I will make all your enemies turn their backs to you.

(Exodus 23:28)

And I will send hornets before you, which shall drive out the Hivite, the Canaanite, and the Hittite, from before you.

(Exodus 23:29)

I will not drive them out from before you in one year; lest the land become desolate, and the beast of the field multiply against you.

(Exodus 23:30)

By little and little I will drive them out from before you, until you be increased, and inherit the land.

(Exodus 23:31)

And I will set your bounds from the Red sea even to the sea of the Philistines, and from the desert to the river: for I will deliver the inhabitants of the land into your hand; and you shall drive them out before you.

(Exodus 23:32)

You shall make no covenant with them, nor with their gods.

(Exodus 23:33)

They shall not dwell in your land, lest they make you sin against me: for if you serve their gods, it will surely be a snare to you.

Exodus: Chapter Twenty-Four

(Exodus 24:1)
And he said to Moses, Come up to the LORD, you, and Aaron, Nadab, and Abihu, and seventy of the elders of Israel; and worship you afar off.

(Exodus 24:2)
And Moses alone shall come near the LORD: but they shall not come nigh; neither shall the people go up with him.

(Exodus 24:3)
And Moses came and told the people all the words of the LORD, and all the judgments: and all the people answered with one voice, and said, All the words which the LORD has said will we do.

(Exodus 24:4)
And Moses wrote all the words of the LORD, and rose up early in the morning, and built an altar under the hill, and twelve pillars, according to the twelve tribes of Israel.

(Exodus 24:5)
And he sent young men of the children of Israel, which offered burnt offerings, and sacrificed peace offerings of oxen to the LORD.

(Exodus 24:6)
And Moses took half of the blood, and put it in basins; and half of the blood he sprinkled on the altar.

(Exodus 24:7)

And he took the book of the covenant, and read in the audience of the people: and they said, All that the LORD has said will we do, and be obedient.

(Exodus 24:8)

And Moses took the blood, and sprinkled it on the people, and said, Behold the blood of the covenant, which the LORD has made with you concerning all these words.

(Exodus 24:9)

Then went up Moses, and Aaron, Nadab, and Abihu, and seventy of the elders of Israel:

(Exodus 24:10)

And they saw the God of Israel: and there was under his feet as it were a paved work of a sapphire stone, and as it were the body of heaven in his clearness.

(Exodus 24:11)

And upon the nobles of the children of Israel he laid not his hand: also they saw God, and did eat and drink.

(Exodus 24:12) (Jubilees 1:1)

And it came to pass in the first year of the exodus of the children of Israel out of Egypt, in the third month, on the sixteenth day of the month, that the LORD God said to Moses, Come up to me into the mount, and be there: and I will give you two tables of stone, and a law, and commandments which I have written; that you may teach them.

(Exodus 24:13)

And Moses rose up, and his minister Joshua: and Moses went up into the mount of God.

(Exodus 24:14)

And he said to the elders, Tarry you here for us, until we come again to you: and, behold, Aaron and Hur are with you: if any man have any matters to do, let him come to them.

(Exodus 24:15) (Jubilees 1:2...)

And Moses went up into the mount, and a cloud covered the mount.

(Exodus 24:16) (Jasher 82:8...) (...Jubilees 1:2, 3...)

And the glory of the LORD abode upon mount Sinai, and the cloud covered it six days: and the seventh day he called to Moses out of the midst of the cloud.

(Exodus 24:17) (...Jubilees 1:3)

And the sight of the glory of the LORD was like devouring fire on the top of the mount in the eyes of the children of Israel.

(Exodus 24:18) (...Jasher 82:8, 9) (Jubilees 1:4)

And Moses went into the midst of the cloud, and ascended up into the mount: and Moses was in the mount forty days and forty nights; he ate no bread and drank no water, and the Lord instructed him in the statutes and judgments in order to teach the children of Israel, and God taught him the earlier and the later history of the division of all the days of the law and of the testimony.

(Jubilees 1:5)

And He said: Incline your heart to every word which I shall speak to you on this mount, and write them in a book in order that their generations may see how I have not forsaken them for all the evil which they have wrought in transgressing the covenant which I establish between Me and you for their generations this day on Mount Sinai.

(Jubilees 1:6)
And thus it will come to pass when all these things come on them, that they will recognize that I am more righteous than they in all their judgments and in all their actions, and they will recognize that I have been truly with them.

(Jubilees 1:7)
And write for yourself all these words which I declare unto, you this day, for I know their rebellion and their stiff neck, before I bring them into the land of which I swore to their fathers, to Abraham and to Isaac and to Jacob, saying: Unto your seed will I give a land flowing with milk and honey.

(Jubilees 1:8)
And they will eat and be satisfied, and they will turn to strange gods, to gods which cannot deliver them from aught of their tribulation: and this witness shall be heard for a witness against them. For they will forget all My commandments, all that I command them, and they will walk after the Gentiles, and after their uncleanness, and after their shame, and will serve their gods, and these will prove unto them an offence and a tribulation and an affliction and a snare.

(Jubilees 1:9)
And many will perish and they will be taken captive, and will fall into the hands of the enemy, because they have forsaken My ordinances and My commandments, and the festivals of My covenant, and My sabbaths, and My holy place which I have hallowed for Myself in their midst, and My tabernacle, and My sanctuary, which I have hallowed for Myself in the midst of the land, that I should set my name on it, and that it should dwell there.

(Jubilees 1:10)
And they will make to themselves high places and groves and

graven images, and they will worship, each his own graven image, so as to go astray, and they will sacrifice their children to demons, and to all the works of the error of their hearts.

(Jubilees 1:11)
And I will send witnesses unto them, that I may witness against them, but they will not hear, and will slay the witnesses also, and they will persecute those who seek the law, and they will abrogate and change everything so as to work evil before My eyes.

(Jubilees 1:12)
And I will hide My face from them, and I will deliver them into the hand of the Gentiles for captivity, and for a prey, and for devouring, and I will remove them from the midst of the land, and I will scatter them amongst the Gentiles.

(Jubilees 1:13)
And they will forget all My law and all My commandments and all My judgments, and will go astray as to new moons, and sabbaths, and festivals, and jubilees, and ordinances.

(Jubilees 1:14)
And after this they will turn to Me from amongst the Gentiles with all their heart and with all their soul and with all their strength, and I will gather them from amongst all the Gentiles, and they will seek me, so that I shall be found of them, when they seek me with all their heart and with all their soul.

(Jubilees 1:15)
And I will disclose to them abounding peace with righteousness, and I will remove them the plant of uprightness, with all My heart and with all My soul, and they shall be for a blessing and not for a curse, and they shall be the head and not the tail.

(Jubilees 1:16)
And I will build My sanctuary in their midst, and I will dwell with them, and I will be their God and they shall be My people in truth and righteousness.

(Jubilees 1:17)
And I will not forsake them nor fail them; for I am the Lord their God.

(Jubilees 1:18)
And Moses fell on his face and prayed and said, O Lord my God, do not forsake Your people and Your inheritance, so that they should wander in the error of their hearts, and do not deliver them into the hands of their enemies, the Gentiles, lest they should rule over them and cause them to sin against You.

(Jubilees 1:19)
Let your mercy, O Lord, be lifted up on Your people, and create in them an upright spirit, and let not the spirit of Beliar rule over them to accuse them before You, and to ensnare them from all the paths of righteousness, so that they may perish from before Your face.

(Jubilees 1:20)
But they are Your people and Your inheritance, which you have delivered with your great power from the hands of the Egyptians: create in them a clean heart and a holy spirit, and let them not be ensnared in their sins from here after, until eternity.

(Jubilees 1:21)
And the Lord said unto Moses: I know their contrariness and their thoughts and their stiffneckedness, and they will not be

obedient till they confess their own sin and the sin of their fathers.

(Jubilees 1:22)
And after this they will turn to Me in all uprightness and with all their heart and with all their soul, and I will circumcise the foreskin of their heart and the foreskin of the heart of their seed, and I will create in them a holy spirit, and I will cleanse them so that they shall not turn away from Me from that day unto eternity.

(Jubilees 1:23)
And their souls will cleave to Me and to all My commandments, and they will fulfill My commandments, and I will be their Father and they shall be My children.

(Jubilees 1:24)
And they all shall be called children of the living God, and every angel and every spirit shall know, yea, they shall know that these are My children, and that I am their Father in uprightness and righteousness, and that I love them.

(Jubilees 1:25)
And do you write down for yourself all these words which I declare unto you on this mountain, the first and the last, which shall come to pass in all the divisions of the days in the law and in the testimony and in the weeks and the jubilees unto eternity, until I descend and dwell with them throughout eternity.

(Jubilees 1:26)
And He said to the angel of the presence: Write for Moses from the beginning of creation till My sanctuary has been built among them for all eternity.

(Jubilees 1:27)
And the Lord will appear to the eyes of all, and all shall know that I am the God of Israel and the Father of all the children of Jacob, and King on Mount Zion for all eternity. And Zion and Jerusalem shall be holy.

(Jubilees 1:28)
And the angel of the presence who went before the camp of Israel took the tables of the divisions of the years - from the time of the creation - of the law and of the testimony of the weeks of the jubilees, according to the individual years, according to all the number of the jubilees according, to the individual years, from the day of the new creation when the heavens and the earth shall be renewed and all their creation according to the powers of the heaven, and according to all the creation of the earth, until the sanctuary of the Lord shall be made in Jerusalem on Mount Zion, and all the luminaries be renewed for healing and for peace and for blessing for all the elect of Israel, and that thus it may be from that day and unto all the days of the earth.

Exodus: Chapter Twenty-Five

(Exodus 25:1)
And the LORD spoke to Moses, saying,

(Exodus 25:2)
Speak to the children of Israel, that they bring me an offering: of every man that gives it willingly with his heart you shall take my offering.

(Exodus 25:3)
And this is the offering which you shall take of them; gold, and silver, and brass,

(Exodus 25:4)
And blue, and purple, and scarlet, and fine linen, and goats' hair,

(Exodus 25:5)
And rams' skins dyed red, and badgers' skins, and shittim wood,

(Exodus 25:6)
Oil for the light, spices for anointing oil, and for sweet incense,

(Exodus 25:7)
Onyx stones, and stones to be set in the ephod, and in the breastplate.

(Exodus 25:8)

And let them make me a sanctuary; that I may dwell among them.

(Exodus 25:9)

According to all that I shew you, after the pattern of the tabernacle, and the pattern of all the instruments thereof, even so shall you make it.

(Exodus 25:10)

And they shall make an ark of shittim wood: two cubits and a half shall be the length thereof, and a cubit and a half the breadth thereof, and a cubit and a half the height thereof.

(Exodus 25:11)

And you shall overlay it with pure gold, within and without shall you overlay it, and shall make upon it a crown of gold round about.

(Exodus 25:12)

And you shall cast four rings of gold for it, and put them in the four corners thereof; and two rings shall be in the one side of it, and two rings in the other side of it.

(Exodus 25:13)

And you shall make staves of shittim wood, and overlay them with gold.

(Exodus 25:14)

And you shall put the staves into the rings by the sides of the ark, that the ark may be borne with them.

(Exodus 25:15)

The staves shall be in the rings of the ark: they shall not be taken from it.

(Exodus 25:16)
And you shall put into the ark the testimony which I shall give you.

(Exodus 25:17)
And you shall make a mercy seat of pure gold: two cubits and a half shall be the length thereof, and a cubit and a half the breadth thereof.

(Exodus 25:18)
And you shall make two cherubims of gold, of beaten work shall you make them, in the two ends of the mercy seat.

(Exodus 25:19)
And make one cherub on the one end, and the other cherub on the other end: even of the mercy seat shall you make the cherubims on the two ends thereof.

(Exodus 25:20)
And the cherubims shall stretch forth their wings on high, covering the mercy seat with their wings, and their faces shall look one to another; toward the mercy seat shall the faces of the cherubims be.

(Exodus 25:21)
And you shall put the mercy seat above upon the ark; and in the ark you shall put the testimony that I shall give you.

(Exodus 25:22)
And there I will meet with you, and I will commune with you from above the mercy seat, from between the two cherubims

which are upon the ark of the testimony, of all things which I will give you in commandment to the children of Israel.

(Exodus 25:23)

You shall also make a table of shittim wood: two cubits shall be the length thereof, and a cubit the breadth thereof, and a cubit and a half the height thereof.

(Exodus 25:24)

And you shall overlay it with pure gold, and make thereto a crown of gold round about.

(Exodus 25:25)

And you shall make to it a border of a hand breadth round about, and you shall make a golden crown to the border thereof round about.

(Exodus 25:26)

And you shall make for it four rings of gold, and put the rings in the four corners that are on the four feet thereof.

(Exodus 25:27)

Over against the border shall the rings be for places of the staves to bear the table.

(Exodus 25:28)

And you shall make the staves of shittim wood, and overlay them with gold, that the table may be borne with them.

(Exodus 25:29)

And you shall make the dishes thereof, and spoons thereof, and covers thereof, and bowls thereof, to cover withal: of pure gold shall you make them.

(Exodus 25:30)

And you shall set upon the table shewbread before me always.

(Exodus 25:31)

And you shall make a candlestick of pure gold: of beaten work shall the candlestick be made: his shaft, and his branches, his bowls, his knops, and his flowers, shall be of the same.

(Exodus 25:32)

And six branches shall come out of the sides of it; three branches of the candlestick out of the one side, and three branches of the candlestick out of the other side:

(Exodus 25:33)

Three bowls made like to almonds, with a knop and a flower in one branch; and three bowls made like almonds in the other branch, with a knop and a flower: so in the six branches that come out of the candlestick.

(Exodus 25:34)

And in the candlestick shall be four bowls made like to almonds, with their knops and their flowers.

(Exodus 25:35)

And there shall be a knop under two branches of the same, and a knop under two branches of the same, and a knop under two branches of the same, according to the six branches that proceed out of the candlestick.

(Exodus 25:36)

Their knops and their branches shall be of the same: all it shall be one beaten work of pure gold.

(Exodus 25:37)

And you shall make the seven lamps thereof: and they shall light the lamps thereof, that they may give light over against it.

(Exodus 25:38)

And the tongs thereof, and the snuff dishes thereof, shall be of pure gold.

(Exodus 25:39)

Of a talent of pure gold shall he make it, with all these vessels.

(Exodus 25:40)

And look that you make them after their pattern, which was shewed you in the mount.

Exodus: Chapter Twenty-Six

(Exodus 26:1)
Moreover you shall make the tabernacle with ten curtains of fine twined linen, and blue, and purple, and scarlet: with cherubims of cunning work shall you make them.

(Exodus 26:2)
The length of one curtain shall be eight and twenty cubits, and the breadth of one curtain four cubits: and every one of the curtains shall have one measure.

(Exodus 26:3)
The five curtains shall be coupled together one to another; and other five curtains shall be coupled one to another.

(Exodus 26:4)
And you shall make loops of blue upon the edge of the one curtain from the selvedge in the coupling; and likewise shall you make in the uttermost edge of another curtain, in the coupling of the second.

(Exodus 26:5)
Fifty loops shall you make in the one curtain, and fifty loops shall you make in the edge of the curtain that is in the coupling of the second; that the loops may take hold one of another.

(Exodus 26:6)
And you shall make fifty taches of gold, and couple the curtains together with the taches: and it shall be one tabernacle.

(Exodus 26:7)

And you shall make curtains of goats' hair to be a covering upon the tabernacle: eleven curtains shall you make.

(Exodus 26:8)

The length of one curtain shall be thirty cubits, and the breadth of one curtain four cubits: and the eleven curtains shall be all of one measure.

(Exodus 26:9)

And you shall couple five curtains by themselves, and six curtains by themselves, and shall double the sixth curtain in the forefront of the tabernacle.

(Exodus 26:10)

And you shall make fifty loops on the edge of the one curtain that is outmost in the coupling, and fifty loops in the edge of the curtain which couples the second.

(Exodus 26:11)

And you shall make fifty taches of brass, and put the taches into the loops, and couple the tent together, that it may be one.

(Exodus 26:12)

And the remnant that remains of the curtains of the tent, the half curtain that remains, shall hang over the backside of the tabernacle.

(Exodus 26:13)

And a cubit on the one side, and a cubit on the other side of that which remains in the length of the curtains of the tent, it shall hang over the sides of the tabernacle on this side and on that side, to cover it.

(Exodus 26:14)
And you shall make a covering for the tent of rams' skins dyed red, and a covering above of badgers' skins.

(Exodus 26:15)
And you shall make boards for the tabernacle of shittim wood standing up.

(Exodus 26:16)
Ten cubits shall be the length of a board, and a cubit and a half shall be the breadth of one board.

(Exodus 26:17)
Two tenons shall there be in one board, set in order one against another: thus shall you make for all the boards of the tabernacle.

(Exodus 26:18)
And you shall make the boards for the tabernacle, twenty boards on the south side southward.

(Exodus 26:19)
And you shall make forty sockets of silver under the twenty boards; two sockets under one board for his two tenons, and two sockets under another board for his two tenons.

(Exodus 26:20)
And for the second side of the tabernacle on the north side there shall be twenty boards:

(Exodus 26:21)
And their forty sockets of silver; two sockets under one board, and two sockets under another board.

(Exodus 26:22)
And for the sides of the tabernacle westward you shall make six boards.

(Exodus 26:23)
And two boards shall you make for the corners of the tabernacle in the two sides.

(Exodus 26:24)
And they shall be coupled together beneath, and they shall be coupled together above the head of it to one ring: thus shall it be for them both; they shall be for the two corners.

(Exodus 26:25)
And they shall be eight boards, and their sockets of silver, sixteen sockets; two sockets under one board, and two sockets under another board.

(Exodus 26:26)
And you shall make bars of shittim wood; five for the boards of the one side of the tabernacle,

(Exodus 26:27)
And five bars for the boards of the other side of the tabernacle, and five bars for the boards of the side of the tabernacle, for the two sides westward.

(Exodus 26:28)
And the middle bar in the midst of the boards shall reach from end to end.

(Exodus 26:29)
And you shall overlay the boards with gold, and make their

rings of gold for places for the bars: and you shall overlay the bars with gold.

(Exodus 26:30)
And you shall rear up the tabernacle according to the fashion thereof which was shewed you in the mount.

(Exodus 26:31)
And you shall make a veil of blue, and purple, and scarlet, and fine twined linen of cunning work: with cherubims shall it be made:

(Exodus 26:32)
And you shall hang it upon four pillars of shittim wood overlaid with gold: their hooks shall be of gold, upon the four sockets of silver.

(Exodus 26:33)
And you shall hang up the veil under the taches, that you may bring in there within the veil the ark of the testimony: and the veil shall divide to you between the holy place and the most holy.

(Exodus 26:34)
And you shall put the mercy seat upon the ark of the testimony in the most holy place.

(Exodus 26:35)
And you shall set the table without the veil, and the candlestick over against the table on the side of the tabernacle toward the south: and you shall put the table on the north side.

(Exodus 26:36)
And you shall make a hanging for the door of the tent, of blue,

and purple, and scarlet, and fine twined linen, wrought with needlework.

(Exodus 26:37)

And you shall make for the hanging five pillars of shittim wood, and overlay them with gold, and their hooks shall be of gold: and you shall cast five sockets of brass for them.

Exodus: Chapter Twenty-Seven

(Exodus 27:1)
And you shall make an altar of shittim wood, five cubits long, and five cubits broad; the altar shall be foursquare: and the height thereof shall be three cubits.

(Exodus 27:2)
And you shall make the horns of it upon the four corners thereof: his horns shall be of the same: and you shall overlay it with brass.

(Exodus 27:3)
And you shall make his pans to receive his ashes, and his shovels, and his basins, and his flesh hooks, and his firepans: all the vessels thereof you shall make of brass.

(Exodus 27:4)
And you shall make for it a grate of network of brass; and upon the net shall you make four brazen rings in the four corners thereof.

(Exodus 27:5)
And you shall put it under the compass of the altar beneath, that the net may be even to the midst of the altar.

(Exodus 27:6)
And you shall make staves for the altar, staves of shittim wood, and overlay them with brass.

(Exodus 27:7)

And the staves shall be put into the rings, and the staves shall be upon the two sides of the altar, to bear it.

(Exodus 27:8)

Hollow with boards shall you make it: as it was shewed you in the mount, so shall they make it.

(Exodus 27:9)

And you shall make the court of the tabernacle: for the south side southward there shall be hangings for the court of fine twined linen of an hundred cubits long for one side:

(Exodus 27:10)

And the twenty pillars thereof and their twenty sockets shall be of brass; the hooks of the pillars and their fillets shall be of silver.

(Exodus 27:11)

And likewise for the north side in length there shall be hangings of an hundred cubits long, and his twenty pillars and their twenty sockets of brass; the hooks of the pillars and their fillets of silver.

(Exodus 27:12)

And for the breadth of the court on the west side shall be hangings of fifty cubits: their pillars ten, and their sockets ten.

(Exodus 27:13)

And the breadth of the court on the east side eastward shall be fifty cubits.

(Exodus 27:14)

The hangings of one side of the gate shall be fifteen cubits: their pillars three, and their sockets three.

(Exodus 27:15)

And on the other side shall be hangings fifteen cubits: their pillars three, and their sockets three.

(Exodus 27:16)

And for the gate of the court shall be a hanging of twenty cubits, of blue, and purple, and scarlet, and fine twined linen, wrought with needlework: and their pillars shall be four, and their sockets four.

(Exodus 27:17)

All the pillars round about the court shall be filleted with silver; their hooks shall be of silver, and their sockets of brass.

(Exodus 27:18)

The length of the court shall be a hundred cubits, and the breadth fifty everywhere, and the height five cubits of fine twined linen, and their sockets of brass.

(Exodus 27:19)

All the vessels of the tabernacle in all the service thereof, and all the pins thereof, and all the pins of the court, shall be of brass.

(Exodus 27:20)

And you shall command the children of Israel, that they bring you pure oil olive beaten for the light, to cause the lamp to burn always.

(Exodus 27:21)

In the tabernacle of the congregation without the veil, which is before the testimony, Aaron and his sons shall order it from evening to morning before the LORD: it shall be a statute forever to their generations on the behalf of the children of Israel.

Exodus: Chapter Twenty-Eight

(Exodus 28:1)

And take you to you Aaron your brother, and his sons with him, from among the children of Israel, that he may minister to me in the priest's office, even Aaron, Nadab and Abihu, Eleazar and Ithamar, Aaron's sons.

(Exodus 28:2)

And you shall make holy garments for Aaron your brother for glory and for beauty.

(Exodus 28:3)

And you shall speak to all that are wise hearted, whom I have filled with the spirit of wisdom, that they may make Aaron's garments to consecrate him, that he may minister to me in the priest's office.

(Exodus 28:4)

And these are the garments which they shall make; a breastplate, and an ephod, and a robe, and a embroidered coat, a mitre, and a girdle: and they shall make holy garments for Aaron your brother, and his sons, that he may minister to me in the priest's office.

(Exodus 28:5)

And they shall take gold, and blue, and purple, and scarlet, and fine linen.

(Exodus 28:6)

And they shall make the ephod of gold, of blue, and of purple, of scarlet, and fine twined linen, with cunning work.

(Exodus 28:7)

It shall have the two shoulder pieces thereof joined at the two edges thereof; and so it shall be joined together.

(Exodus 28:8)

And the curious girdle of the ephod, which is upon it, shall be of the same, according to the work thereof; even of gold, of blue, and purple, and scarlet, and fine twined linen.

(Exodus 28:9)

And you shall take two onyx stones, and grave on them the names of the children of Israel:

(Exodus 28:10)

Six of their names on one stone, and the other six names of the rest on the other stone, according to their birth.

(Exodus 28:11)

With the work of an engraver in stone, like the engravings of a signet, shall you engrave the two stones with the names of the children of Israel: you shall make them to be set in ouches of gold.

(Exodus 28:12)

And you shall put the two stones upon the shoulders of the ephod for stones of memorial to the children of Israel: and Aaron shall bear their names before the LORD upon his two shoulders for a memorial.

(Exodus 28:13)

And you shall make ouches of gold;

(Exodus 28:14)

And two chains of pure gold at the ends; of wreathen work shall you make them, and fasten the wreathen chains to the ouches.

(Exodus 28:15)

And you shall make the breastplate of judgment with cunning work; after the work of the ephod you shall make it; of gold, of blue, and of purple, and of scarlet, and of fine twined linen, shall you make it.

(Exodus 28:16)

Foursquare it shall be being doubled; a span shall be the length thereof, and a span shall be the breadth thereof.

(Exodus 28:17)

And you shall set in it settings of stones, even four rows of stones: the first row shall be a sardius, a topaz, and a carbuncle: this shall be the first row.

(Exodus 28:18)

And the second row shall be an emerald, a sapphire, and a diamond.

(Exodus 28:19)

And the third row a ligure, an agate, and an amethyst.

(Exodus 28:20)

And the fourth row a beryl, and an onyx, and a jasper: they shall be set in gold in their enclosings.

(Exodus 28:21)

And the stones shall be with the names of the children of

Israel, twelve, according to their names, like the engravings of a signet; everyone with his name shall they be according to the twelve tribes.

(Exodus 28:22)

And you shall make upon the breastplate chains at the ends of wreathen work of pure gold.

(Exodus 28:23)

And you shall make upon the breastplate two rings of gold, and shall put the two rings on the two ends of the breastplate.

(Exodus 28:24)

And you shall put the two wreathen chains of gold in the two rings which are on the ends of the breastplate.

(Exodus 28:25)

And the other two ends of the two wreathen chains you shall fasten in the two ouches, and put them on the shoulder pieces of the ephod before it.

(Exodus 28:26)

And you shall make two rings of gold, and you shall put them upon the two ends of the breastplate in the border thereof, which is in the side of the ephod inward.

(Exodus 28:27)

And two other rings of gold you shall make, and shall put them on the two sides of the ephod underneath, toward the forepart thereof, over against the other coupling thereof, above the curious girdle of the ephod.

(Exodus 28:28)

And they shall bind the breastplate by the rings thereof to the rings of the ephod with a lace of blue, that it may be above the curious girdle of the ephod, and that the breastplate be not loosed from the ephod.

(Exodus 28:29)

And Aaron shall bear the names of the children of Israel in the breastplate of judgment upon his heart, when he goes in to the holy place, for a memorial before the LORD continually.

(Exodus 28:30)

And you shall put in the breastplate of judgment the Urim and the Thummim; and they shall be upon Aaron's heart, when he goes in before the LORD: and Aaron shall bear the judgment of the children of Israel upon his heart before the LORD continually.

(Exodus 28:31)

And you shall make the robe of the ephod all of blue.

(Exodus 28:32)

And there shall be an hole in the top of it, in the midst thereof: it shall have a binding of woven work round about the hole of it, as it were the hole of an habergeon, that it be not rent.

(Exodus 28:33)

And beneath upon the hem of it you shall make pomegranates of blue, and of purple, and of scarlet, round about the hem thereof; and bells of gold between them round about:

(Exodus 28:34)

A golden bell and a pomegranate, a golden bell and a pomegranate, upon the hem of the robe round about.

(Exodus 28:35)

And it shall be upon Aaron to minister: and his sound shall be heard when he goes in to the holy place before the LORD, and when he comes out, that he dies not.

(Exodus 28:36)

And you shall make a plate of pure gold, and grave upon it, like the engravings of a signet, HOLINESS TO THE LORD.

(Exodus 28:37)

And you shall put it on a blue lace, that it may be upon the mitre; upon the forefront of the mitre it shall be.

(Exodus 28:38)

And it shall be upon Aaron's forehead, that Aaron may bear the iniquity of the holy things, which the children of Israel shall hallow in all their holy gifts; and it shall be always upon his forehead, that they may be accepted before the LORD.

(Exodus 28:39)

And you shall embroider the coat of fine linen, and you shall make the mitre of fine linen, and you shall make the girdle of needlework.

(Exodus 28:40)

And for Aaron's sons you shall make coats, and you shall make for them girdles, and bonnets shall you make for them, for glory and for beauty.

(Exodus 28:41)

And you shall put them upon Aaron your brother, and his sons with him; and shall anoint them, and consecrate them, and sanctify them, that they may minister to me in the priest's office.

(Exodus 28:42)

And you shall make them linen breeches to cover their nakedness; from the loins even to the thighs they shall reach:

(Exodus 28:43)

And they shall be upon Aaron, and upon his sons, when they come in to the tabernacle of the congregation, or when they come near to the altar to minister in the holy place; that they bear not iniquity, and die: it shall be a statute forever to him and his seed after him.

Exodus: Chapter Twenty-Nine

(Exodus 29:1)
And this is the thing that you shall do to them to hallow them, to minister to me in the priest's office: Take one young bullock, and two rams without blemish,

(Exodus 29:2)
And unleavened bread, and cakes unleavened tempered with oil, and wafers unleavened anointed with oil: of wheaten flour shall you make them.

(Exodus 29:3)
And you shall put them into one basket, and bring them in the basket, with the bullock and the two rams.

(Exodus 29:4)
And Aaron and his sons you shall bring to the door of the tabernacle of the congregation, and shall wash them with water.

(Exodus 29:5)
And you shall take the garments, and put upon Aaron the coat, and the robe of the ephod, and the ephod, and the breastplate, and gird him with the curious girdle of the ephod:

(Exodus 29:6)
And you shall put the mitre upon his head, and put the holy crown upon the mitre.

(Exodus 29:7)
Then shall you take the anointing oil, and pour it upon his head, and anoint him.

(Exodus 29:8)
And you shall bring his sons, and put coats upon them.

(Exodus 29:9)
And you shall gird them with girdles, Aaron and his sons, and put the bonnets on them: and the priest's office shall be theirs for a perpetual statute: and you shall consecrate Aaron and his sons.

(Exodus 29:10)
And you shall cause a bullock to be brought before the tabernacle of the congregation: and Aaron and his sons shall put their hands upon the head of the bullock.

(Exodus 29:11)
And you shall kill the bullock before the LORD, by the door of the tabernacle of the congregation.

(Exodus 29:12)
And you shall take of the blood of the bullock, and put it upon the horns of the altar with your finger, and pour all the blood beside the bottom of the altar.

(Exodus 29:13)
And you shall take all the fat that covers the inwards, and the caul that is above the liver, and the two kidneys, and the fat that is upon them, and burn them upon the altar.

(Exodus 29:14)
But the flesh of the bullock, and his skin, and his dung, shall

you burn with fire without the camp: it is a sin offering.

(Exodus 29:15)
You shall also take one ram; and Aaron and his sons shall put their hands upon the head of the ram.

(Exodus 29:16)
And you shall slay the ram, and you shall take his blood, and sprinkle it round about upon the altar.

(Exodus 29:17)
And you shall cut the ram in pieces, and wash the inwards of him, and his legs, and put them to his pieces, and to his head.

(Exodus 29:18)
And you shall burn the whole ram upon the altar: it is a burnt offering to the LORD: it is a sweet savor, an offering made by fire to the LORD.

(Exodus 29:19)
And you shall take the other ram; and Aaron and his sons shall put their hands upon the head of the ram.

(Exodus 29:20)
Then shall you kill the ram, and take of his blood, and put it upon the tip of the right ear of Aaron, and upon the tip of the right ear of his sons, and upon the thumb of their right hand, and upon the great toe of their right foot, and sprinkle the blood upon the altar round about.

(Exodus 29:21)
And you shall take of the blood that is upon the altar, and of the anointing oil, and sprinkle it upon Aaron, and upon his garments, and upon his sons, and upon the garments of his

sons with him: and he shall be hallowed, and his garments, and his sons, and his sons' garments with him.

(Exodus 29:22)

Also you shall take of the ram the fat and the rump, and the fat that covers the inwards, and the caul above the liver, and the two kidneys, and the fat that is upon them, and the right shoulder; for it is a ram of consecration:

(Exodus 29:23)

And one loaf of bread, and one cake of oiled bread, and one wafer out of the basket of the unleavened bread that is before the LORD:

(Exodus 29:24)

And you shall put all in the hands of Aaron, and in the hands of his sons; and shall wave them for a wave offering before the LORD.

(Exodus 29:25)

And you shall receive them of their hands, and burn them upon the altar for a burnt offering, for a sweet savor before the LORD: it is an offering made by fire to the LORD.

(Exodus 29:26)

And you shall take the breast of the ram of Aaron's consecration, and wave it for a wave offering before the LORD: and it shall be your part.

(Exodus 29:27)

And you shall sanctify the breast of the wave offering, and the shoulder of the heave offering, which is waved, and which is heaved up, of the ram of the consecration, even of that which is for Aaron, and of that which is for his sons:

(Exodus 29:28)

And it shall be Aaron's and his sons' by a statute forever from the children of Israel: for it is an heave offering: and it shall be an heave offering from the children of Israel of the sacrifice of their peace offerings, even their heave offering to the LORD.

(Exodus 29:29)

And the holy garments of Aaron shall be his sons' after him, to be anointed therein, and to be consecrated in them.

(Exodus 29:30)

And that son that is priest in his stead shall put them on seven days, when he comes into the tabernacle of the congregation to minister in the holy place.

(Exodus 29:31)

And you shall take the ram of the consecration, and seethe his flesh in the holy place.

(Exodus 29:32)

And Aaron and his sons shall eat the flesh of the ram, and the bread that is in the basket, by the door of the tabernacle of the congregation.

(Exodus 29:33)

And they shall eat those things wherewith the atonement was made, to consecrate and to sanctify them: but a stranger shall not eat thereof, because they are holy.

(Exodus 29:34)

And if ought of the flesh of the consecrations, or of the bread, remain to the morning, then you shall burn the remainder with fire: it shall not be eaten, because it is holy.

(Exodus 29:35)

And thus shall you do to Aaron, and to his sons, according to all things which I have commanded you: seven days shall you consecrate them.

(Exodus 29:36)

And you shall offer every day a bullock for a sin offering for atonement: and you shall cleanse the altar, when you have made an atonement for it, and you shall anoint it, to sanctify it.

(Exodus 29:37)

Seven days you shall make an atonement for the altar, and sanctify it; and it shall be an altar most holy: whatsoever touches the altar shall be holy.

(Exodus 29:38)

Now this is that which you shall offer upon the altar; two lambs of the first year day by day continually.

(Exodus 29:39)

The one lamb you shall offer in the morning; and the other lamb you shall offer at even:

(Exodus 29:40)

And with the one lamb a tenth deal of flour mingled with the fourth part of an hin of beaten oil; and the fourth part of an hin of wine for a drink offering.

(Exodus 29:41)

And the other lamb you shall offer at even, and shall do thereto according to the meat offering of the morning, and according to the drink offering thereof, for a sweet savor, an offering made by fire to the LORD.

(Exodus 29:42)

This shall be a continual burnt offering throughout your generations at the door of the tabernacle of the congregation before the LORD: where I will meet you, to speak there to you.

(Exodus 29:43)

And there I will meet with the children of Israel, and the tabernacle shall be sanctified by my glory.

(Exodus 29:44)

And I will sanctify the tabernacle of the congregation, and the altar: I will sanctify also both Aaron and his sons, to minister to me in the priest's office.

(Exodus 29:45)

And I will dwell among the children of Israel, and will be their God.

(Exodus 29:46)

And they shall know that I am the LORD their God, that brought them forth out of the land of Egypt, that I may dwell among them: I am the LORD their God.

Exodus: Chapter Thirty

(Exodus 30:1)
And you shall make an altar to burn incense upon: of shittim wood shall you make it.

(Exodus 30:2)
A cubit shall be the length thereof, and a cubit the breadth thereof; foursquare shall it be: and two cubits shall be the height thereof: the horns thereof shall be of the same.

(Exodus 30:3)
And you shall overlay it with pure gold, the top thereof, and the sides thereof round about, and the horns thereof; and you shall make to it a crown of gold round about.

(Exodus 30:4)
And two golden rings shall you make to it under the crown of it, by the two corners thereof, upon the two sides of it shall you make it; and they shall be for places for the staves to bear it withal.

(Exodus 30:5)
And you shall make the staves of shittim wood, and overlay them with gold.

(Exodus 30:6)
And you shall put it before the veil that is by the ark of the testimony, before the mercy seat that is over the testimony, where I will meet with you.

(Exodus 30:7)

And Aaron shall burn thereon sweet incense every morning: when he dresses the lamps, he shall burn incense upon it.

(Exodus 30:8)

And when Aaron lights the lamps at even, he shall burn incense upon it, a perpetual incense before the LORD throughout your generations.

(Exodus 30:9)

You shall offer no strange incense thereon, nor burnt sacrifice, nor meat offering; neither shall you pour drink offering thereon.

(Exodus 30:10)

And Aaron shall make an atonement upon the horns of it once in a year with the blood of the sin offering of atonements: once in the year shall he make atonement upon it throughout your generations: it is most holy to the LORD.

(Exodus 30:11)

And the LORD spoke to Moses, saying,

(Exodus 30:12)

When you take the sum of the children of Israel after their number, then shall they give every man a ransom for his soul to the LORD, when you number them; that there be no plague among them, when you number them.

(Exodus 30:13)

This they shall give, every one that passes among them that are numbered, half a shekel after the shekel of the sanctuary: (a shekel is twenty gerahs:) an half shekel shall be the offering of the LORD.

(Exodus 30:14)
Every one that passes among them that are numbered, from twenty years old and above, shall give an offering to the LORD.

(Exodus 30:15)
The rich shall not give more, and the poor shall not give less than half a shekel, when they give an offering to the LORD, to make an atonement for your souls.

(Exodus 30:16)
And you shall take the atonement money of the children of Israel, and shall appoint it for the service of the tabernacle of the congregation; that it may be a memorial to the children of Israel before the LORD, to make an atonement for your souls.

(Exodus 30:17)
And the LORD spoke to Moses, saying,

(Exodus 30:18)
You shall also make a laver of brass, and his foot also of brass, to wash withal: and you shall put it between the tabernacle of the congregation and the altar, and you shall put water therein.

(Exodus 30:19)
For Aaron and his sons shall wash their hands and their feet thereat:

(Exodus 30:20)
When they go into the tabernacle of the congregation, they shall wash with water, that they die not; or when they come near to the altar to minister, to burn offering made by fire to the LORD:

(Exodus 30:21)
So they shall wash their hands and their feet, that they die not: and it shall be a statute forever to them, even to him and to his seed throughout their generations.

(Exodus 30:22)
Moreover the LORD spoke to Moses, saying,

(Exodus 30:23)
Take you also to you principal spices, of pure myrrh five hundred shekels, and of sweet cinnamon half so much, even two hundred and fifty shekels, and of sweet calamus two hundred and fifty shekels,

(Exodus 30:24)
And of cassia five hundred shekels, after the shekel of the sanctuary, and of oil olive an hin:

(Exodus 30:25)
And you shall make it an oil of holy ointment, an ointment compound after the are of the apothecary: it shall be an holy anointing oil.

(Exodus 30:26)
And you shall anoint the tabernacle of the congregation therewith, and the ark of the testimony,

(Exodus 30:27)
And the table and all his vessels, and the candlestick and his vessels, and the altar of incense,

(Exodus 30:28)
And the altar of burnt offering with all his vessels, and the laver and his foot.

(Exodus 30:29)

And you shall sanctify them, that they may be most holy: whatsoever touches them shall be holy.

(Exodus 30:30)

And you shall anoint Aaron and his sons, and consecrate them, that they may minister to me in the priest's office.

(Exodus 30:31)

And you shall speak to the children of Israel, saying, This shall be an holy anointing oil to me throughout your generations.

(Exodus 30:32)

Upon man's flesh shall it not be poured, neither shall you make any other like it, after the composition of it: it is holy, and it shall be holy to you.

(Exodus 30:33)

Whosoever compounds any like it, or whosoever puts any of it upon a stranger, shall even be cut off from his people.

(Exodus 30:34)

And the LORD said to Moses, Take to you sweet spices, stacte, and onycha, and galbanum; these sweet spices with pure frankincense: of each shall there be a like weight:

(Exodus 30:35)

And you shall make it a perfume, a confection after the are of the apothecary, tempered together, pure and holy:

(Exodus 30:36)

And you shall beat some of it very small, and put of it before the testimony in the tabernacle of the congregation, where I will meet with you: it shall be to you most holy.

(Exodus 30:37)

And as for the perfume which you shall make, you shall not make to yourselves according to the composition thereof: it shall be to you holy for the LORD.

(Exodus 30:38)

Whosoever shall make like to that, to smell thereto, shall even be cut off from his people.

Exodus: Chapter Thirty-One

(Exodus 31:1)
And the LORD spoke to Moses, saying,

(Exodus 31:2)
See, I have called by name Bezaleel the son of Uri, the son of Hur, of the tribe of Judah:

(Exodus 31:3)
And I have filled him with the spirit of God, in wisdom, and in understanding, and in knowledge, and in all manner of workmanship,

(Exodus 31:4)
To devise cunning works, to work in gold, and in silver, and in brass,

(Exodus 31:5)
And in cutting of stones, to set them, and in carving of timber, to work in all manner of workmanship.

(Exodus 31:6)
And I, behold, I have given with him Aholiab, the son of Ahisamach, of the tribe of Dan: and in the hearts of all that are wise hearted I have put wisdom, that they may make all that I have commanded you;

(Exodus 31:7)
The tabernacle of the congregation, and the ark of the

testimony, and the mercy seat that is thereupon, and all the furniture of the tabernacle,

(Exodus 31:8)
And the table and his furniture, and the pure candlestick with all his furniture, and the altar of incense,

(Exodus 31:9)
And the altar of burnt offering with all his furniture, and the laver and his foot,

(Exodus 31:10)
And the cloths of service, and the holy garments for Aaron the priest, and the garments of his sons, to minister in the priest's office,

(Exodus 31:11)
And the anointing oil, and sweet incense for the holy place: according to all that I have commanded you shall they do.

(Exodus 31:12)
And the LORD spoke to Moses, saying,

(Exodus 31:13)
Speak you also to the children of Israel, saying, Verily my sabbaths you shall keep: for it is a sign between me and you throughout your generations; that you may know that I am the LORD that does sanctify you.

(Exodus 31:14)
You shall keep the sabbath therefore; for it is holy to you: every one that defiles it shall surely be put to death: for whosoever does any work therein, that soul shall be cut off from among his people.

(Exodus 31:15)

Six days may work be done; but in the seventh is the sabbath of rest, holy to the LORD: whosoever does any work in the sabbath day, he shall surely be put to death.

(Exodus 31:16)

Why the children of Israel shall keep the sabbath, to observe the sabbath throughout their generations, for a perpetual covenant.

(Exodus 31:17)

It is a sign between me and the children of Israel forever: for in six days the LORD made heaven and earth, and on the seventh day he rested, and was refreshed.

(Jasher 82:10)

And the Lord wrote the ten commandments which he had commanded the children of Israel upon two tablets of stone, which he gave to Moses to command the children of Israel.

(Exodus 31:18) (Jasher 82:11)

And at the end of forty days and forty nights, he gave to Moses, when he had made an end of communing with him upon mount Sinai, two tables of testimony, tables of stone, written with the finger of God.

Exodus: Chapter Thirty-Two

(Exodus 32:1) (Jasher 82:12, 13)

And when the people saw that Moses delayed to come down out of the mount, the people gathered themselves together to Aaron, and said to him, Up, make us gods, which shall go before us, so that you shall not die; for as for this Moses, the man that brought us up out of the land of Egypt, we do not know what is become of him.

(Exodus 32:2) (Jasher 82:14...)

And Aaron was greatly afraid of the people, and he ordered them to bring him gold and said to them, Break off the golden earrings, which are in the ears of your wives, of your sons, and of your daughters, and bring them to me.

(Exodus 32:3)

And all the people brake off the golden earrings which were in their ears, and brought them to Aaron.

(Exodus 32:4) (...Jasher 82:14)

And he received them at their hand, and fashioned it with a graving tool, after he had made it a molten calf: and they said, These be your gods, O Israel, which brought you up out of the land of Egypt.

(Exodus 32:5)

And when Aaron saw it, he built an altar before it; and Aaron made proclamation, and said, Tomorrow is a feast to the LORD.

(Exodus 32:6)

And they rose up early on the morrow, and offered burnt offerings, and brought peace offerings; and the people sat down to eat and to drink, and rose up to play.

(Exodus 32:7) (Jasher 82:15)

And the LORD said to Moses, before he had come down from the mount, Go, get down; for your people, which you brought out of the land of Egypt, have corrupted themselves:

(Exodus 32:8) (Jasher 82:16...)

They have turned aside quickly out of the way which I commanded them: they have made them a molten calf, and have bowed down to it, and have worshipped it, and have sacrificed thereunto, and said, These be your gods, O Israel, which have brought you up out of the land of Egypt.

(Exodus 32:9)

And the LORD said to Moses, I have seen this people, and, behold, it is a stiff necked people:

(Exodus 32:10) (...Jasher 82:16)

Now therefore let me alone, that my wrath may wax hot against them, and that I may consume them from off the earth, for they are a stiffnecked people: and I will make of you a great nation.

(Exodus 32:11) (Jasher 82:17...)

And Moses besought the countenance of the LORD his God, and he prayed to the Lord for the people on account of the calf which they had made, and said, LORD, why does your wrath wax hot against your people, which you have brought forth out of the land of Egypt with great power, and with a mighty hand?

(Exodus 32:12)

Why should the Egyptians speak, and say, For mischief did he bring them out, to slay them in the mountains, and to consume them from the face of the earth? Turn from your fierce wrath, and repent of this evil against your people.

(Exodus 32:13)

Remember Abraham, Isaac, and Israel, your servants, to whom you swore by your own self, and said to them, I will multiply your seed as the stars of heaven, and all this land that I have spoken of will I give to your seed, and they shall inherit it forever.

(Exodus 32:14)

And the LORD repented of the evil which he thought to do to his people.

(Exodus 32:15) (...Jasher 82:17)

And Moses afterward turned, and went down from the mount, and the two tables of the testimony were in his hand: the tables were written on both their sides; on the one side and on the other were they written, which God had given him to command the Israelites.

(Exodus 32:16)

And the tables were the work of God, and the writing was the writing of God, graven upon the tables.

(Exodus 32:17)

And when Joshua heard the noise of the people as they shouted, he said to Moses, There is a noise of war in the camp.

(Exodus 32:18)

And he said, It is not the voice of them that shout for mastery, neither is it the voice of them that cry for being overcome: but the noise of them that sing do I hear.

(Exodus 32:19) (Jasher 82:18)

And it came to pass, as soon as he came nigh to the camp, that he saw the calf which the people had made, and the dancing: and Moses' anger waxed hot, and he cast the tables out of his hands, and brake them beneath the mount.

(Exodus 32:20) (Jasher 82:19)

And Moses came to the camp and he took the calf which they had made, and burnt it in the fire, and ground it to powder, and strewed it upon the water, and made the children of Israel drink of it.

(Exodus 32:21)

And Moses said to Aaron, What did this people to you, that you have brought so great a sin upon them?

(Exodus 32:22)

And Aaron said, Let not the anger of my lord wax hot: you know the people, that they are set on mischief.

(Exodus 32:23)

For they said to me, Make us gods, which shall go before us: for as for this Moses, the man that brought us up out of the land of Egypt, we wot not what is become of him.

(Exodus 32:24)

And I said to them, Whosoever has any gold, let them break it off. So they gave it me: then I cast it into the fire, and there came out this calf.

(Exodus 32:25)

And when Moses saw that the people were naked; (for Aaron had made them naked to their shame among their enemies:)

(Exodus 32:26)

Then Moses stood in the gate of the camp, and said, Who is on the LORD'S side? Let him come to me. And all the sons of Levi gathered themselves together to him.

(Exodus 32:27)

And he said to them, Thus says the LORD God of Israel, Put every man his sword by his side, and go in and out from gate to gate throughout the camp, and slay every man his brother, and every man his companion, and every man his neighbor.

(Exodus 32:28) (Jasher 82:20)

And the children of Levi did according to the word of Moses: and there fell of the people that day by the swords of each other about three thousand men who had made the calf.

(Exodus 32:29)

For Moses had said, Consecrate yourselves today to the LORD, even every man upon his son, and upon his brother; that he may bestow upon you a blessing this day.

(Exodus 32:30) (Jasher 82:21)

And it came to pass on the morrow, that Moses said to the people, You have sinned a great sin: and now I will go up to the LORD; peradventure I shall make an atonement for your sin which you have sinned to the Lord.

(Exodus 32:31) (Jasher 82:22...)

And Moses returned to the LORD, and said, Oh, this people have sinned a great sin, and have made them gods of gold.

(Exodus 32:32)
Yet now, if you will forgive their sin--; and if not, blot me, I pray you, out of your book which you have written.

(...Jasher 82:22)
And he remained with the Lord forty days and forty nights.

(Jasher 82:23)
And during the forty days did Moses entreat the Lord in behalf of the children of Israel, and the Lord hearkened to the prayer of Moses, and the Lord was entreated of him in behalf of Israel.

(Exodus 32:33)
And the LORD said to Moses, Whosoever has sinned against me, him will I blot out of my book.

(Exodus 32:34)
Therefore now go, lead the people to the place of which I have spoken to you: behold, mine Angel shall go before you: nevertheless in the day when I visit I will visit their sin upon them.

(Exodus 32:35)
And the LORD plagued the people, because they made the calf, which Aaron made.

Exodus: Chapter Thirty-Three

(Exodus 33:1)

And the LORD said to Moses, Depart, and go up hence, you and the people which you have brought up out of the land of Egypt, to the land which I swore to Abraham, to Isaac, and to Jacob, saying, To your seed will I give it:

(Exodus 33:2)

And I will send an angel before you; and I will drive out the Canaanite, the Amorite, and the Hittite, and the Perizzite, the Hivite, and the Jebusite:

(Exodus 33:3)

To a land flowing with milk and honey: for I will not go up in the midst of you; for you are a stiff necked people: lest I consume you in the way.

(Exodus 33:4)

And when the people heard these evil tidings, they mourned: and no man did put on him his ornaments.

(Exodus 33:5)

For the LORD had said to Moses, Say to the children of Israel, You are a stiff necked people: I will come up into the midst of you in a moment, and consume you: therefore now put off your ornaments from you, that I may know what to do to you.

(Exodus 33:6)

And the children of Israel stripped themselves of their ornaments by the mount Horeb.

(Exodus 33:7)

And Moses took the tabernacle, and pitched it without the camp, afar off from the camp, and called it the Tabernacle of the congregation. And it came to pass, that every one which sought the LORD went out to the tabernacle of the congregation, which was without the camp.

(Exodus 33:8)

And it came to pass, when Moses went out to the tabernacle, that all the people rose up, and stood every man at his tent door, and looked after Moses, until he was gone into the tabernacle.

(Exodus 33:9)

And it came to pass, as Moses entered into the tabernacle, the cloudy pillar descended, and stood at the door of the tabernacle, and the LORD talked with Moses.

(Exodus 33:10)

And all the people saw the cloudy pillar stand at the tabernacle door: and all the people rose up and worshipped, every man in his tent door.

(Exodus 33:11)

And the LORD spoke to Moses face to face, as a man speaks to his friend. And he turned again into the camp: but his servant Joshua, the son of Nun, a young man, departed not out of the tabernacle.

(Exodus 33:12)

And Moses said to the LORD, See, you say to me, Bring up this people: and you have not let me know whom you will send with me. Yet you have said, I know you by name, and you have also found grace in my sight.

(Exodus 33:13)

Now therefore, I pray you, if I have found grace in your sight, shew me now your way, that I may know you, that I may find grace in your sight: and consider that this nation is your people.

(Exodus 33:14)

And he said, My presence shall go with you, and I will give you rest.

(Exodus 33:15)

And he said to him, If your presence goes not with me, carry us not up hence.

(Exodus 33:16)

For wherein shall it be known here that I and your people have found grace in your sight? Is it not in that you go with us? So shall we be separated, I and your people, from all the people that are upon the face of the earth.

(Exodus 33:17)

And the LORD said to Moses, I will do this thing also that you have spoken: for you have found grace in my sight, and I know you by name.

(Exodus 33:18)

And he said, I beseech you, shew me your glory.

(Exodus 33:19)

And he said, I will make all my goodness pass before you, and I will proclaim the name of the LORD before you; and will be gracious to whom I will be gracious, and will shew mercy on whom I will shew mercy.

(Exodus 33:20)

And he said, You can not see my face: for there shall no man see me, and live.

(Exodus 33:21)

And the LORD said, Behold, there is a place by me, and you shall stand upon a rock:

(Exodus 33:22)

And it shall come to pass, while my glory passes by, that I will put you in a clift of the rock, and will cover you with my hand while I pass by:

(Exodus 33:23)

And I will take away mine hand, and you shall see my back parts: but my face shall not be seen.

Exodus: Chapter Thirty-Four

(Exodus 34:1) (Jasher 82:24)

And the LORD said to Moses, Hew you two tables of stone like to the first and to bring them up to the Lord, and I will write upon these tables the words that were in the first tables, the ten commandments, which you broke.

(Exodus 34:2)

And be ready in the morning, and come up in the morning to mount Sinai, and present yourself there to me in the top of the mount.

(Exodus 34:3)

And no man shall come up with you, neither let any man be seen throughout all the mount; neither let the flocks nor herds feed before that mount.

(Exodus 34:4) (Jasher 82:25...)

And now Moses did so, and he came down and he hewed two tables of stone like to the first; and Moses rose up early in the morning, and went up to mount Sinai to the Lord, as the LORD had commanded him, and took in his hand the two tables of stone.

(Exodus 34:5)

And the LORD descended in the cloud, and stood with him there, and proclaimed the name of the LORD.

(Exodus 34:6)

And the LORD passed by before him, and proclaimed, The

LORD, The LORD God, merciful and gracious, longsuffering, and abundant in goodness and truth,

(Exodus 34:7)

Keeping mercy for thousands, forgiving iniquity and transgression and sin, and that will by no means clear the guilty; visiting the iniquity of the fathers upon the children, and upon the children's children, to the third and to the fourth generation.

(Exodus 34:8)

And Moses made haste, and bowed his head toward the earth, and worshipped.

(Exodus 34:9)

And he said, If now I have found grace in your sight, O Lord, let my Lord, I pray you, go among us; for it is a stiff necked people; and pardon our iniquity and our sin, and take us for your inheritance.

(...Jasher 82:25)

And the Lord wrote the ten commandments upon the tablets.

(Exodus 34:10)

And he said, Behold, I make a covenant: before all your people I will do marvels, such as have not been done in all the earth, nor in any nation: and all the people among which you are shall see the work of the LORD: for it is a terrible thing that I will do with you.

(Exodus 34:11)

Observe you that which I command you this day: behold, I drive out before you the Amorite, and the Canaanite, and the Hittite, and the Perizzite, and the Hivite, and the Jebusite.

(Exodus 34:12)

Take heed to yourself, lest you make a covenant with the inhabitants of the land where you go, lest it be for a snare in the midst of you:

(Exodus 34:13)

But you shall destroy their altars, break their images, and cut down their groves:

(Exodus 34:14)

For you shall worship no other god: for the LORD, whose name is Jealous, is a jealous God:

(Exodus 34:15)

Lest you make a covenant with the inhabitants of the land, and they go a whoring after their gods, and do sacrifice to their gods, and one call you, and you eat of his sacrifice;

(Exodus 34:16)

And you take of their daughters to your sons, and their daughters go a whoring after their gods, and make your sons go a whoring after their gods.

(Exodus 34:17)

You shall make you no molten gods.

(Exodus 34:18)

The feast of unleavened bread shall you keep. Seven days you shall eat unleavened bread, as I commanded you, in the time of the month Abib: for in the month Abib you came out from Egypt.

(Exodus 34:19)

All that opens the matrix is mine; and every firstling among your cattle, whether ox or sheep, that is male.

(Exodus 34:20)

But the firstling of an donkey you shall redeem with a lamb: and if you redeem him not, then shall you break his neck. All the firstborn of your sons you shall redeem. And none shall appear before me empty.

(Exodus 34:21)

Six days you shall work, but on the seventh day you shall rest: in earing time and in harvest you shall rest.

(Exodus 34:22)

And you shall observe the feast of weeks, of the firstfruits of wheat harvest, and the feast of ingathering at the year's end.

(Exodus 34:23)

Thrice in the year shall all your men children appear before the Lord GOD, the God of Israel.

(Exodus 34:24)

For I will cast out the nations before you, and enlarge your borders: neither shall any man desire your land, when you shall go up to appear before the LORD your God thrice in the year.

(Exodus 34:25)

You shall not offer the blood of my sacrifice with leaven; neither shall the sacrifice of the feast of the passover be left to the morning.

(Exodus 34:26)

The first of the firstfruits of your land you shall bring to the house of the LORD your God. You shall not seethe a kid in his mother's milk.

(Exodus 34:27)

And the LORD said to Moses, Write these words: for after the tenor of these words I have made a covenant with you and with Israel.

(Exodus 34:28) (...Jasher 82:25, 26)

And he was there with the LORD forty days and forty nights; he did neither eat bread, nor drink water. And the Lord wrote upon the tables the words of the covenant, the ten commandments, and the Lord instructed him in statutes and judgments to impart to Israel.

(Jasher 82:27)

And the Lord commanded him respecting the children of Israel that they should make a sanctuary for the Lord, that his name might rest therein, and the Lord showed him the likeness of the sanctuary and the likeness of all its vessels.

(Exodus 34:29) (Jasher 82:28)

And it came to pass, at the end of the forty days, when Moses came down from mount Sinai with the two tables of testimony in Moses' hand, when he came down from the mount, that Moses knew not that the skin of his face shone while he talked with him.

(Exodus 34:30)

And when Aaron and all the children of Israel saw Moses, behold, the skin of his face shone; and they were afraid to come nigh him.

(Exodus 34:31)

And Moses called to them; and Aaron and all the rulers of the congregation returned to him: and Moses talked with them.

(Exodus 34:32) (Jasher 82:29)

And afterward Moses came to the children of Israel and all the children of Israel came nigh: and he gave them in commandment all that the LORD had spoken with him in mount Sinai, and he taught them laws, statutes and judgments which the Lord had taught him.

(Exodus 34:33)

And till Moses had done speaking with them, he put a veil on his face.

(Exodus 34:34)

But when Moses went in before the LORD to speak with him, he took the veil off, until he came out. And he came out, and spoke to the children of Israel that which he was commanded.

(Exodus 34:35)

And the children of Israel saw the face of Moses, that the skin of Moses' face shone: and Moses put the veil upon his face again, until he went in to speak with him.

Exodus: Chapter Thirty-Five

(Exodus 35:1)
And Moses gathered all the congregation of the children of Israel together, and said to them, These are the words which the LORD has commanded, that you should do them.

(Exodus 35:2)
Six days shall work be done, but on the seventh day there shall be to you a holy day, a sabbath of rest to the LORD: whosoever does work therein shall be put to death.

(Exodus 35:3)
You shall kindle no fire throughout your habitations upon the sabbath day.

(Jasher 82:30)
And Moses told the children of Israel the word of the Lord, that a sanctuary should be made for him, to dwell among the children of Israel.

(Exodus 35:4)
And Moses spoke to all the congregation of the children of Israel, saying, This is the thing which the LORD commanded, saying,

(Exodus 35:5)
Take you from among you an offering to the LORD: whosoever is of a willing heart, let him bring it, an offering of the LORD; gold, and silver, and brass,

(Exodus 35:6)
And blue, and purple, and scarlet, and fine linen, and goats' hair,

(Exodus 35:7)
And rams' skins dyed red, and badgers' skins, and shittim wood,

(Exodus 35:8)
And oil for the light, and spices for anointing oil, and for the sweet incense,

(Exodus 35:9)
And onyx stones, and stones to be set for the ephod, and for the breastplate.

(Exodus 35:10)
And every wise hearted among you shall come, and make all that the LORD has commanded;

(Exodus 35:11)
The tabernacle, his tent, and his covering, his taches, and his boards, his bars, his pillars, and his sockets,

(Exodus 35:12)
The ark, and the staves thereof, with the mercy seat, and the veil of the covering,

(Exodus 35:13)
The table, and his staves, and all his vessels, and the shewbread,

(Exodus 35:14)
The candlestick also for the light, and his furniture, and his

lamps, with the oil for the light,

(Exodus 35:15)
And the incense altar, and his staves, and the anointing oil, and the sweet incense, and the hanging for the door at the entering in of the tabernacle,

(Exodus 35:16)
The altar of burnt offering, with his brazen grate, his staves, and all his vessels, the laver and his foot,

(Exodus 35:17)
The hangings of the court, his pillars, and their sockets, and the hanging for the door of the court,

(Exodus 35:18)
The pins of the tabernacle, and the pins of the court, and their cords,

(Exodus 35:19)
The cloths of service, to do service in the holy place, the holy garments for Aaron the priest, and the garments of his sons, to minister in the priest's office.

(Jasher 82:31)
And the people rejoiced greatly at all the good which the Lord had spoken to them, through Moses, and they said, We will do all that the Lord has spoken to you.

(Exodus 35:20)
And all the congregation of the children of Israel departed from the presence of Moses.

(Exodus 35:21) (Jasher 82:32)
And the people rose up like one man and they came, every one whose heart stirred him up, and every one whom his spirit made willing, and they made generous offerings to the sanctuary of the Lord, and each man brought the LORD'S offering to the work of the tabernacle of the congregation, and for all his service, and for the holy garments.

(Jasher 82:33)
And all the children of Israel brought each man of all that was found in his possession for the work of the sanctuary of the Lord, gold, silver and brass, and every thing that was serviceable for the sanctuary.

(Exodus 35:22)
And they came, both men and women, as many as were willing hearted, and brought bracelets, and earrings, and rings, and tablets, all jewels of gold: and every man that offered an offering of gold to the LORD.

(Exodus 35:23)
And every man, with whom was found blue, and purple, and scarlet, and fine linen, and goats' hair, and red skins of rams, and badgers' skins, brought them.

(Exodus 35:24)
Every one that did offer an offering of silver and brass brought the LORD'S offering: and every man, with whom was found shittim wood for any work of the service, brought it.

(Exodus 35:25)
And all the women that were wise hearted did spin with their hands, and brought that which they had spun, both of blue, and of purple, and of scarlet, and of fine linen.

(Exodus 35:26)
And all the women whose heart stirred them up in wisdom spun goats' hair.

(Exodus 35:27)
And the rulers brought onyx stones, and stones to be set, for the ephod, and for the breastplate;

(Exodus 35:28)
And spice, and oil for the light, and for the anointing oil, and for the sweet incense.

(Exodus 35:29)
The children of Israel brought a willing offering to the LORD, every man and woman, whose heart made them willing to bring for all manner of work, which the LORD had commanded to be made by the hand of Moses.

(Exodus 35:30)
And Moses said to the children of Israel, See, the LORD has called by name Bezaleel the son of Uri, the son of Hur, of the tribe of Judah;

(Exodus 35:31)
And he has filled him with the spirit of God, in wisdom, in understanding, and in knowledge, and in all manner of workmanship;

(Exodus 35:32)
And to devise curious works, to work in gold, and in silver, and in brass,

(Exodus 35:33)
And in the cutting of stones, to set them, and in carving of

wood, to make any manner of cunning work.

(Exodus 35:34)

And he has put in his heart that he may teach, both he, and Aholiab, the son of Ahisamach, of the tribe of Dan.

(Exodus 35:35)

Them has he filled with wisdom of heart, to work all manner of work, of the engraver, and of the cunning workman, and of the embroiderer, in blue, and in purple, in scarlet, and in fine linen, and of the weaver, even of them that do any work, and of those that devise cunning work.

Exodus: Chapter Thirty-Six

(Exodus 36:1)

Then wrought Bezaleel and Aholiab, and every wise hearted man, in whom the LORD put wisdom and understanding to know how to work all manner of work for the service of the sanctuary, according to all that the LORD had commanded.

(Exodus 36:2)

And Moses called Bezaleel and Aholiab, and every wise hearted man, in whose heart the LORD had put wisdom, even every one whose heart stirred him up to come to the work to do it:

(Exodus 36:3)

And they received of Moses all the offering, which the children of Israel had brought for the work of the service of the sanctuary, to make it withal. And they brought yet to him free offerings every morning.

(Exodus 36:4) (Jasher 82:34)

And all the wise men who were practiced in work, that wrought all the work of the sanctuary, came every man from his work which they made, and made the sanctuary of the Lord, according to all that the Lord had commanded, every man in the work in which he had been practiced; and all the wise men in heart made the sanctuary, and its furniture and all the vessels for the holy service, as the Lord had commanded Moses.

(Exodus 36:5)

And they spoke to Moses, saying, The people bring much more than enough for the service of the work, which the LORD commanded to make.

(Exodus 36:6)

And Moses gave commandment, and they caused it to be proclaimed throughout the camp, saying, Let neither man nor woman make any more work for the offering of the sanctuary. So the people were restrained from bringing.

(Exodus 36:7)

For the stuff they had was sufficient for all the work to make it, and too much.

(Exodus 36:8)

And every wise hearted man among them that wrought the work of the tabernacle made ten curtains of fine twined linen, and blue, and purple, and scarlet: with cherubims of cunning work made he them.

(Exodus 36:9)

The length of one curtain was twenty and eight cubits, and the breadth of one curtain four cubits: the curtains were all of one size.

(Exodus 36:10)

And he coupled the five curtains one to another: and the other five curtains he coupled one to another.

(Exodus 36:11)

And he made loops of blue on the edge of one curtain from the selvedge in the coupling: likewise he made in the uttermost side of another curtain, in the coupling of the second.

(Exodus 36:12)

Fifty loops made he in one curtain, and fifty loops made he in the edge of the curtain which was in the coupling of the second: the loops held one curtain to another.

(Exodus 36:13)

And he made fifty taches of gold, and coupled the curtains one to another with the taches: so it became one tabernacle.

(Exodus 36:14)

And he made curtains of goats' hair for the tent over the tabernacle: eleven curtains he made them.

(Exodus 36:15)

The length of one curtain was thirty cubits, and four cubits was the breadth of one curtain: the eleven curtains were of one size.

(Exodus 36:16)

And he coupled five curtains by themselves, and six curtains by themselves.

(Exodus 36:17)

And he made fifty loops upon the uttermost edge of the curtain in the coupling, and fifty loops made he upon the edge of the curtain which couples the second.

(Exodus 36:18)

And he made fifty taches of brass to couple the tent together, that it might be one.

(Exodus 36:19)

And he made a covering for the tent of rams' skins dyed red, and a covering of badgers' skins above that.

(Exodus 36:20)
And he made boards for the tabernacle of shittim wood, standing up.

(Exodus 36:21)
The length of a board was ten cubits, and the breadth of a board one cubit and a half.

(Exodus 36:22)
One board had two tenons, equally distant one from another: thus did he make for all the boards of the tabernacle.

(Exodus 36:23)
And he made boards for the tabernacle; twenty boards for the south side southward:

(Exodus 36:24)
And forty sockets of silver he made under the twenty boards; two sockets under one board for his two tenons, and two sockets under another board for his two tenons.

(Exodus 36:25)
And for the other side of the tabernacle, which is toward the north corner, he made twenty boards,

(Exodus 36:26)
And their forty sockets of silver; two sockets under one board, and two sockets under another board.

(Exodus 36:27)
And for the sides of the tabernacle westward he made six boards.

(Exodus 36:28)

And two boards made he for the corners of the tabernacle in the two sides.

(Exodus 36:29)

And they were coupled beneath, and coupled together at the head thereof, to one ring: thus he did to both of them in both the corners.

(Exodus 36:30)

And there were eight boards; and their sockets were sixteen sockets of silver, under every board two sockets.

(Exodus 36:31)

And he made bars of shittim wood; five for the boards of the one side of the tabernacle,

(Exodus 36:32)

And five bars for the boards of the other side of the tabernacle, and five bars for the boards of the tabernacle for the sides westward.

(Exodus 36:33)

And he made the middle bar to shoot through the boards from the one end to the other.

(Exodus 36:34)

And he overlaid the boards with gold, and made their rings of gold to be places for the bars, and overlaid the bars with gold.

(Exodus 36:35)

And he made a veil of blue, and purple, and scarlet, and fine twined linen: with cherubims made he it of cunning work.

(Exodus 36:36)

And he made thereunto four pillars of shittim wood, and overlaid them with gold: their hooks were of gold; and he cast for them four sockets of silver.

(Exodus 36:37)

And he made a hanging for the tabernacle door of blue, and purple, and scarlet, and fine twined linen, of needlework;

(Exodus 36:38)

And the five pillars of it with their hooks: and he overlaid their chapiters and their fillets with gold: but their five sockets were of brass.

Exodus: Chapter Thirty-Seven

(Exodus 37:1)
And Bezaleel made the ark of shittim wood: two cubits and a half was the length of it, and a cubit and a half the breadth of it, and a cubit and a half the height of it:

(Exodus 37:2)
And he overlaid it with pure gold within and without, and made a crown of gold to it round about.

(Exodus 37:3)
And he cast for it four rings of gold, to be set by the four corners of it; even two rings upon the one side of it, and two rings upon the other side of it.

(Exodus 37:4)
And he made staves of shittim wood, and overlaid them with gold.

(Exodus 37:5)
And he put the staves into the rings by the sides of the ark, to bear the ark.

(Exodus 37:6)
And he made the mercy seat of pure gold: two cubits and a half was the length thereof, and one cubit and a half the breadth thereof.

(Exodus 37:7)
And he made two cherubims of gold, beaten out of one piece

made he them, on the two ends of the mercy seat;

(Exodus 37:8)

One cherub on the end on this side, and another cherub on the other end on that side: out of the mercy seat made he the cherubims on the two ends thereof.

(Exodus 37:9)

And the cherubims spread out their wings on high, and covered with their wings over the mercy seat, with their faces one to another; even toward the mercy seat were the faces of the cherubims.

(Exodus 37:10)

And he made the table of shittim wood: two cubits was the length thereof, and a cubit the breadth thereof, and a cubit and a half the height thereof:

(Exodus 37:11)

And he overlaid it with pure gold, and made thereunto a crown of gold round about.

(Exodus 37:12)

Also he made thereunto a border of an handbreadth round about; and made a crown of gold for the border thereof round about.

(Exodus 37:13)

And he cast for it four rings of gold, and put the rings upon the four corners that were in the four feet thereof.

(Exodus 37:14)

Over against the border were the rings, the places for the staves to bear the table.

(Exodus 37:15)

And he made the staves of shittim wood, and overlaid them with gold, to bear the table.

(Exodus 37:16)

And he made the vessels which were upon the table, his dishes, and his spoons, and his bowls, and his covers to cover withal, of pure gold.

(Exodus 37:17)

And he made the candlestick of pure gold: of beaten work made he the candlestick; his shaft, and his branch, his bowls, his knops, and his flowers, were of the same:

(Exodus 37:18)

And six branches going out of the sides thereof; three branches of the candlestick out of the one side thereof, and three branches of the candlestick out of the other side thereof:

(Exodus 37:19)

Three bowls made after the fashion of almonds in one branch, a knop and a flower; and three bowls made like almonds in another branch, a knop and a flower: so throughout the six branches going out of the candlestick.

(Exodus 37:20)

And in the candlestick were four bowls made like almonds, his knops, and his flowers:

(Exodus 37:21)

And a knop under two branches of the same, and a knop under two branches of the same, and a knop under two branches of the same, according to the six branches going out of it.

(Exodus 37:22)

Their knops and their branches were of the same: all of it was one beaten work of pure gold.

(Exodus 37:23)

And he made his seven lamps, and his snuffers, and his snuff dishes, of pure gold.

(Exodus 37:24)

Of a talent of pure gold made he it, and all the vessels thereof.

(Exodus 37:25)

And he made the incense altar of shittim wood: the length of it was a cubit, and the breadth of it a cubit; it was foursquare; and two cubits was the height of it; the horns thereof were of the same.

(Exodus 37:26)

And he overlaid it with pure gold, both the top of it, and the sides thereof round about, and the horns of it: also he made to it a crown of gold round about.

(Exodus 37:27)

And he made two rings of gold for it under the crown thereof, by the two corners of it, upon the two sides thereof, to be places for the staves to bear it withal.

(Exodus 37:28)

And he made the staves of shittim wood, and overlaid them with gold.

(Exodus 37:29)

And he made the holy anointing oil, and the pure incense of sweet spices, according to the work of the apothecary.

Exodus: Chapter Thirty-Eight

(Exodus 38:1)

And he made the altar of burnt offering of shittim wood: five cubits was the length thereof, and five cubits the breadth thereof; it was foursquare; and three cubits the height thereof.

(Exodus 38:2)

And he made the horns thereof on the four corners of it; the horns thereof were of the same: and he overlaid it with brass.

(Exodus 38:3)

And he made all the vessels of the altar, the pots, and the shovels, and the basins, and the fleshhooks, and the firepans: all the vessels thereof made he of brass.

(Exodus 38:4)

And he made for the altar a brazen grate of network under the compass thereof beneath to the midst of it.

(Exodus 38:5)

And he cast four rings for the four ends of the grate of brass, to be places for the staves.

(Exodus 38:6)

And he made the staves of shittim wood, and overlaid them with brass.

(Exodus 38:7)

And he put the staves into the rings on the sides of the altar, to bear it withal; he made the altar hollow with boards.

(Exodus 38:8)

And he made the laver of brass, and the foot of it of brass, of the looking glasses of the women assembling, which assembled at the door of the tabernacle of the congregation.

(Exodus 38:9)

And he made the court: on the south side southward the hangings of the court were of fine twined linen, an hundred cubits:

(Exodus 38:10)

Their pillars were twenty, and their brazen sockets twenty; the hooks of the pillars and their fillets were of silver.

(Exodus 38:11)

And for the north side the hangings were a hundred cubits, their pillars were twenty, and their sockets of brass twenty; the hooks of the pillars and their fillets of silver.

(Exodus 38:12)

And for the west side were hangings of fifty cubits, their pillars ten, and their sockets ten; the hooks of the pillars and their fillets of silver.

(Exodus 38:13)

And for the east side eastward fifty cubits.

(Exodus 38:14)

The hangings of the one side of the gate were fifteen cubits; their pillars three, and their sockets three.

(Exodus 38:15)

And for the other side of the court gate, on this hand and that hand, were hangings of fifteen cubits; their pillars three, and their sockets three.

(Exodus 38:16)
All the hangings of the court round about were of fine twined linen.

(Exodus 38:17)
And the sockets for the pillars were of brass; the hooks of the pillars and their fillets of silver; and the overlaying of their chapiters of silver; and all the pillars of the court were filleted with silver.

(Exodus 38:18)
And the hanging for the gate of the court was needlework, of blue, and purple, and scarlet, and fine twined linen: and twenty cubits was the length, and the height in the breadth was five cubits, answerable to the hangings of the court.

(Exodus 38:19)
And their pillars were four, and their sockets of brass four; their hooks of silver, and the overlaying of their chapiters and their fillets of silver.

(Exodus 38:20)
And all the pins of the tabernacle, and of the court round about, were of brass.

(Exodus 38:21)
This is the sum of the tabernacle, even of the tabernacle of testimony, as it was counted, according to the commandment of Moses, for the service of the Levites, by the hand of Ithamar, son to Aaron the priest.

(Exodus 38:22)

And Bezaleel the son of Uri, the son of Hur, of the tribe of Judah, made all that the LORD commanded Moses.

(Exodus 38:23)

And with him was Aholiab, son of Ahisamach, of the tribe of Dan, an engraver, and a cunning workman, and an embroiderer in blue, and in purple, and in scarlet, and fine linen.

(Exodus 38:24)

All the gold that was occupied for the work in all the work of the holy place, even the gold of the offering, was twenty and nine talents, and seven hundred and thirty shekels, after the shekel of the sanctuary.

(Exodus 38:25)

And the silver of them that were numbered of the congregation was a hundred talents, and a thousand seven hundred and threescore and fifteen shekels, after the shekel of the sanctuary:

(Exodus 38:26)

A bekah for every man, that is, half a shekel, after the shekel of the sanctuary, for every one that went to be numbered, from twenty years old and upward, for six hundred thousand and three thousand and five hundred and fifty men.

(Exodus 38:27)

And of the hundred talents of silver were cast the sockets of the sanctuary, and the sockets of the veil; a hundred sockets of the hundred talents, a talent for a socket.

(Exodus 38:28)

And of the thousand seven hundred seventy and five shekels he made hooks for the pillars, and overlaid their chapiters, and filleted them.

(Exodus 38:29)

And the brass of the offering was seventy talents, and two thousand and four hundred shekels.

(Exodus 38:30)

And therewith he made the sockets to the door of the tabernacle of the congregation, and the brazen altar, and the brazen grate for it, and all the vessels of the altar,

(Exodus 38:31)

And the sockets of the court round about, and the sockets of the court gate, and all the pins of the tabernacle, and all the pins of the court round about.

Exodus: Chapter Thirty-Nine

(Exodus 39:1)

And of the blue, and purple, and scarlet, they made cloths of service, to do service in the holy place, and made the holy garments for Aaron; as the LORD commanded Moses.

(Exodus 39:2)

And he made the ephod of gold, blue, and purple, and scarlet, and fine twined linen.

(Exodus 39:3)

And they did beat the gold into thin plates, and cut it into wires, to work it in the blue, and in the purple, and in the scarlet, and in the fine linen, with cunning work.

(Exodus 39:4)

They made shoulder pieces for it, to couple it together: by the two edges was it coupled together.

(Exodus 39:5)

And the curious girdle of his ephod, that was upon it, was of the same, according to the work thereof; of gold, blue, and purple, and scarlet, and fine twined linen; as the LORD commanded Moses.

(Exodus 39:6)

And they wrought onyx stones enclosed in ouches of gold, graven, as signets are graven, with the names of the children of Israel.

(Exodus 39:7)

And he put them on the shoulders of the ephod, that they should be stones for a memorial to the children of Israel; as the LORD commanded Moses.

(Exodus 39:8)

And he made the breastplate of cunning work, like the work of the ephod; of gold, blue, and purple, and scarlet, and fine twined linen.

(Exodus 39:9)

It was foursquare; they made the breastplate double: a span was the length thereof, and a span the breadth thereof, being doubled.

(Exodus 39:10)

And they set in it four rows of stones: the first row was a sardius, a topaz, and a carbuncle: this was the first row.

(Exodus 39:11)

And the second row, an emerald, a sapphire, and a diamond.

(Exodus 39:12)

And the third row, a ligure, an agate, and an amethyst.

(Exodus 39:13)

And the fourth row, a beryl, an onyx, and a jasper: they were enclosed in ouches of gold in their enclosings.

(Exodus 39:14)

And the stones were according to the names of the children of Israel, twelve, according to their names, like the engravings of a signet, every one with his name, according to the twelve tribes.

(Exodus 39:15)

And they made upon the breastplate chains at the ends, of wreathen work of pure gold.

(Exodus 39:16)

And they made two ouches of gold, and two gold rings; and put the two rings in the two ends of the breastplate.

(Exodus 39:17)

And they put the two wreathen chains of gold in the two rings on the ends of the breastplate.

(Exodus 39:18)

And the two ends of the two wreathen chains they fastened in the two ouches, and put them on the shoulder pieces of the ephod, before it.

(Exodus 39:19)

And they made two rings of gold, and put them on the two ends of the breastplate, upon the border of it, which was on the side of the ephod inward.

(Exodus 39:20)

And they made two other golden rings, and put them on the two sides of the ephod underneath, toward the forepart of it, over against the other coupling thereof, above the curious girdle of the ephod.

(Exodus 39:21)

And they did bind the breastplate by his rings to the rings of the ephod with a lace of blue, that it might be above the curious girdle of the ephod, and that the breastplate might not be loosed from the ephod; as the LORD commanded Moses.

(Exodus 39:22)
And he made the robe of the ephod of woven work, all of blue.

(Exodus 39:23)
And there was a hole in the midst of the robe, as the hole of an habergeon, with a band round about the hole, that it should not rend.

(Exodus 39:24)
And they made upon the hems of the robe pomegranates of blue, and purple, and scarlet, and twined linen.

(Exodus 39:25)
And they made bells of pure gold, and put the bells between the pomegranates upon the hem of the robe, round about between the pomegranates;

(Exodus 39:26)
A bell and a pomegranate, a bell and a pomegranate, round about the hem of the robe to minister in; as the LORD commanded Moses.

(Exodus 39:27)
And they made coats of fine linen of woven work for Aaron, and for his sons,

(Exodus 39:28)
And a mitre of fine linen, and goodly bonnets of fine linen, and linen breeches of fine twined linen,

(Exodus 39:29)
And a girdle of fine twined linen, and blue, and purple, and scarlet, of needlework; as the LORD commanded Moses.

(Exodus 39:30)

And they made the plate of the holy crown of pure gold, and wrote upon it a writing, like to the engravings of a signet, HOLINESS TO THE LORD.

(Exodus 39:31)

And they tied to it a lace of blue, to fasten it on high upon the mitre; as the LORD commanded Moses.

(Exodus 39:32) (Jasher 82:35)

Thus was all the work of the tabernacle of the tent of the congregation finished at the end of five months: and the children of Israel did according to all that the LORD commanded Moses, so did they.

(Exodus 39:33) (Jasher 82:36...)

And they brought the tabernacle to Moses, the tent, and all his furniture, his taches, his boards, his bars, and his pillars, and his sockets,

(Exodus 39:34)

And the covering of rams' skins dyed red, and the covering of badgers' skins, and the veil of the covering,

(Exodus 39:35)

The ark of the testimony, and the staves thereof, and the mercy seat,

(Exodus 39:36)

The table, and all the vessels thereof, and the shewbread,

(Exodus 39:37)

The pure candlestick, with the lamps thereof, even with the

lamps to be set in order, and all the vessels thereof, and the oil for light,

(Exodus 39:38)
And the golden altar, and the anointing oil, and the sweet incense, and the hanging for the tabernacle door,

(Exodus 39:39)
The brazen altar, and his grate of brass, his staves, and all his vessels, the laver and his foot,

(Exodus 39:40)
The hangings of the court, his pillars, and his sockets, and the hanging for the court gate, his cords, and his pins, and all the vessels of the service of the tabernacle, for the tent of the congregation,

(Exodus 39:41)
The cloths of service to do service in the holy place, and the holy garments for Aaron the priest, and his sons' garments, to minister in the priest's office.

(Exodus 39:42) (...Jasher 82:36)
According to all that the LORD commanded Moses, like unto the representation which the Lord had shown to Moses, so the children of Israel made all the work.

(Exodus 39:43) (Jasher 82:37)
And Moses looked upon all the work, and, behold, they had done it as the LORD had commanded him, even so had they done it: and Moses blessed them.

Exodus: Chapter Forty

(Exodus 40:1)
And the LORD spoke to Moses, saying,

(Exodus 40:2)
On the first day of the first month shall you set up the tabernacle of the tent of the congregation.

(Exodus 40:3)
And you shall put therein the ark of the testimony, and cover the ark with the veil.

(Exodus 40:4)
And you shall bring in the table, and set in order the things that are to be set in order upon it; and you shall bring in the candlestick, and light the lamps thereof.

(Exodus 40:5)
And you shall set the altar of gold for the incense before the ark of the testimony, and put the hanging of the door to the tabernacle.

(Exodus 40:6)
And you shall set the altar of the burnt offering before the door of the tabernacle of the tent of the congregation.

(Exodus 40:7)
And you shall set the laver between the tent of the congregation and the altar, and shall put water therein.

(Exodus 40:8)
And you shall set up the court round about, and hang up the hanging at the court gate.

(Exodus 40:9)
And you shall take the anointing oil, and anoint the tabernacle, and all that is therein, and shall hallow it, and all the vessels thereof: and it shall be holy.

(Exodus 40:10)
And you shall anoint the altar of the burnt offering, and all his vessels, and sanctify the altar: and it shall be an altar most holy.

(Exodus 40:11)
And you shall anoint the laver and his foot, and sanctify it.

(Exodus 40:12)
And you shall bring Aaron and his sons to the door of the tabernacle of the congregation, and wash them with water.

(Exodus 40:13)
And you shall put upon Aaron the holy garments, and anoint him, and sanctify him; that he may minister to me in the priest's office.

(Exodus 40:14)
And you shall bring his sons, and clothe them with coats:

(Exodus 40:15)
And you shall anoint them, as you didst anoint their father, that they may minister to me in the priest's office: for their anointing shall surely be an everlasting priesthood throughout their generations.

(Jasher 83:1)
And in the twelfth month, in the twenty-third day of the month, Moses took Aaron and his sons, and he dressed them in their garments, and anointed them and did unto them as the Lord had commanded him, and Moses brought up all the offerings which the Lord had on that day commanded him.

(Exodus 40:16)
Thus did Moses: according to all that the LORD commanded him, so did he.

(Jasher 83:2)
Moses afterward took Aaron and his sons and said to them, For seven days shall you remain at the door of the tabernacle, for thus am I commanded.

(Jasher 83:3)
And Aaron and his sons did all that the Lord had commanded them through Moses, and they remained for seven days at the door of the tabernacle.

(Exodus 40:17) (Jasher 83:4...)
And it came to pass on the eighth day, being in the first month in the second year from the Israelites' departure from Egypt, on the first day of the month, that the tabernacle was reared up.

(Exodus 40:18) (...Jasher 83:4...)
And Moses reared up the tabernacle, and fastened his sockets, and set up the boards thereof, and put in the bars thereof, and reared up his pillars.

(Exodus 40:19)
And he spread abroad the tent over the tabernacle, and put the

covering of the tent above upon it; as the LORD commanded Moses.

(Exodus 40:20)
And he took and put the testimony into the ark, and set the staves on the ark, and put the mercy seat above upon the ark:

(Exodus 40:21)
And he brought the ark into the tabernacle, and set up the veil of the covering, and covered the ark of the testimony; as the LORD commanded Moses.

(Exodus 40:22)
And he put the table in the tent of the congregation, upon the side of the tabernacle northward, without the veil.

(Exodus 40:23)
And he set the bread in order upon it before the LORD; as the LORD had commanded Moses.

(Exodus 40:24)
And he put the candlestick in the tent of the congregation, over against the table, on the side of the tabernacle southward.

(Exodus 40:25)
And he lighted the lamps before the LORD; as the LORD commanded Moses.

(Exodus 40:26)
And he put the golden altar in the tent of the congregation before the veil:

(Exodus 40:27)
And he burnt sweet incense thereon; as the LORD commanded Moses.

(Exodus 40:28)
And he set up the hanging at the door of the tabernacle.

(Exodus 40:29)
And he put the altar of burnt offering by the door of the tabernacle of the tent of the congregation, and offered upon it the burnt offering and the meat offering; as the LORD commanded Moses.

(Exodus 40:30)
And he set the laver between the tent of the congregation and the altar, and put water there, to wash withal.

(...Jasher 83:4)
And Moses put up all the furniture of the tabernacle and all the furniture of the sanctuary, and he did all that the Lord had commanded him.

(Exodus 40:31)
And Moses and Aaron and his sons washed their hands and their feet thereat:

(Exodus 40:32)
When they went into the tent of the congregation, and when they came near to the altar, they washed; as the LORD commanded Moses.

(Exodus 40:33)
And he reared up the court round about the tabernacle and

the altar, and set up the hanging of the court gate. So Moses finished the work.

(Exodus 40:34)

Then a cloud covered the tent of the congregation, and the glory of the LORD filled the tabernacle.

(Exodus 40:35)

And Moses was not able to enter into the tent of the congregation, because the cloud abode thereon, and the glory of the LORD filled the tabernacle.

(Exodus 40:36)

And when the cloud was taken up from over the tabernacle, the children of Israel went onward in all their journeys:

(Exodus 40:37)

But if the cloud were not taken up, then they journeyed not till the day that it was taken up.

(Exodus 40:38)

For the cloud of the LORD was upon the tabernacle by day, and fire was on it by night, in the sight of all the house of Israel, throughout all their journeys.

Final Notes

We hope your journey is enriched and you are blessed through the production of the **Ancient Texts and the Bible** series!

Minister 2 Others would like to hear from you. If you have comments or questions concerning our materials, or if you find errors in our projects, misspellings, or formatting issues. We work hard to provide quality materials, however, sometimes things can squeak by unnoticed. Your feedback is truly appreciated.

We love producing helpful, innovative books and we are grateful for your support! If you have enjoyed this production, please consider writing a review and letting others know about our materials.

If you would like to be updated when we release new books and other materials, please sign up for our e-newsletter on our website.

Thanks!

Minister 2 Others

Minister2others.com

www.ingramcontent.com/pod-product-compliance
Lightning Source LLC
Chambersburg PA
CBHW071814190726
48292CB00008B/2829

* 9 7 8 1 9 4 7 7 5 1 2 5 5 *